Scattering the Proud

CHRISTIANITY BEYOND 2000

Sean O'Conaill

authorHOUSE®

AuthorHouse™
1663 Liberty Drive
Bloomington, IN 47403
www.authorhouse.com
Phone: 1-800-839-8640

Cover by Bill Bolger
The detail from The Stations of the Cross, by Frances Biggs, in St Macartan's Cathedral, Monaghan, is used by kind permission of Bishop Joseph Duffy.

Published by AuthorHouse   07/06/2012

ISBN: 978-1-4685-8558-2 (sc)
ISBN: 978-1-4685-8559-9 (e)

This book is printed on acid-free paper.

For my parents, Vera and Brian, and my wife, Patricia,
whose constancy has been for me a sacrament
of the faithful love of another trinity.

Acknowledgements

In one way or another, the following have all contributed to the matter or spirit of this book. I list them alphabetically because together they have taught me that we are all equally, and infinitely, loved: David Aldred, Norman and Jean Austin, Roger Austin, Richard Beauchesne, Gil Bailie, Jim Biechler, Dave Clare, Bill Cleary, Julia Crozier, The Cursillo community of Derry Diocese, Desmond Daly, Billy Doherty, Charlie Doherty, Ronan Drury, Barbara Duddy, Anne Farrell IBVM, Peter Hunter OP, Betty Irwin, David Jackson, Jim Keener, Maureen Kelly, Nan Kyte, James Lee, The staff and pupils of Loreto College, Coleraine, The sisters of Loreto Convent, Coleraine, Johnny McCallion, Maureen and Nuala McCormick, Michael and Bridie McGoldrick, Schira McGoldrick, Brian McKenna, Gerry and Bernadette McLaughlin, Heber McMahon, Tom McMahon, Tony Mailey and his Christology Class of '99, Klaus Mertes SJ, Janet Millar, Gerry Morrison, Patricia Mullan, Sean O Boyle, James O'Carroll, Aidan O'Conaill, Brian O'Conaill, Cliona O'Conaill, Patricia O'Conaill, Sean G. O'Conaill, Ciaran O'Connell & family, Michael O'Connell & family, Terence and Rosemary Race, Margaret Rafferty, Marceile and Ed Redmon, Ginny Richards, Richard Rohr OFM, Ingrid Shafer, Catherine Stidsen, Leonard Swidler, Michael and Margaret Timoney, Maurice Traynor, Roy Turton, Joe Veale SJ, Bill Watson SJ, Johnny White.

CONTENTS

Introductory Note to first edition (1999)

As this book is intended for the general reader, historical or other terms that might cause problems are explained in a short glossary at the back. Terms such as 'Enlightenment' and 'upward journey' can be found there.

As conventional English still lacks gender-inclusive pronouns, the use of he/she, his/hers, etc., should be understood as referring inclusively to both genders unless the context clearly indicates otherwise.

Introductory Note to second edition (2012)

In 1999 I mistakenly anticipated rapid and radical reform within the Catholic Church, and was over-optimistic about the impact this book might make on that cause in the short term.

However, I have decided not to amend the book accordingly, as its central argument remains sound and relevant, and optimism is not a vice.

In the meantime the dual crisis of western Christianity and western secularism has intensified, and there is increasing readiness to consider radically new mindsets that can somehow add 'passionate intensity' to our deepest convictions and projects, and restore our 'post-modern' optimism. I still hope that this book, and the many supporting articles on my website at www.seanoconaill.com, can yet make a helpful contribution to that cause.

Sean O'Conaill

May 2012

CHAPTER I

The Chasm

'Too many people are falling into the chasm between the word and the deed.'

This observation, placed by Dennis Potter in the mouths of two quite different characters in two different dramas, sums up the experience of many millions of people in the twentieth century.

The first occurrence was in the film *Gorky Park*, in which a Moscow policeman in the Brezhnev era suspected a political dimension to the murder of three people. The chasm of which he spoke was the yawning void between the socialist Eden that communist ideology had promised the Russian people, and the terror it actually delivered. Perhaps thirty million people fell into this murderous abyss in the 20th century, with the lives of several times that number tragically affected. This gulf was so obvious by the late 1980s that the empire built on the hollow promises of Marxism-Leninism came crashing down, with consequences that are still unfolding. The ideology of the free market which took their place in Russia has so far failed to close the chasm between the visionary future and daily reality—due to corruption and organised crime as well as bad planning. The chasm in Russia is now of a different order—but millions are still falling into it, with consequences we cannot yet foresee.

The second of Potter's characters was a member of the anti-Nazi minority in Germany in the mid 1930s. The murderous realities of the Third Reich were by then obvious to liberal and Christian opponents of the system, as they came under increasing pressure from the Gestapo. The

1

glorious thousand-year reich—Hitler's promise—brought twelve years of horror to most of Europe, including genocide to most of Europe's Jews, and left Germany with a burden of shame that still appals its children.

In both cases optimistic ideologies had proven not simply ineffective but murderous on a colossal scale, and so it is important that we understand this term. A political ideology is one that claims to interpret the past correctly, and so claims also the right to determine the future. For Marx, the past was to be interpreted as a battlefield of warring classes, and the future was to be the triumphant global victory of the workers and peasants—represented by the communist party. For Hitler, the past was a conflict of races in which Germany—treacherously betrayed by internal enemies in the war of 1914-18—represented the heroic 'Aryan' race. Under his leadership Germany would create a glorious Aryan empire which would dominate Europe and the western world.

These two ideological chasms, which have overshadowed this century, strongly suggest that we humans are at our most dangerous when we believe we understand everything, and can determine everything. Thoughtful people now seriously question whether any ideology is trustworthy, but ideologies still abound. Ethnic nationalism still transfixes eastern Europe and the Middle East, and the ideology of the market dominates the world's economic systems. Yet here are more chasms for millions. Nationalism promises 'national security' but causes ethnic conflict which uproots and victimises whole communities, and brings atrocities such as Srebrenica and Omagh. The free market does not 'raise all boats' as its most enthusiastic proponents claim. It condemns third world countries to decades of debt redemption, and therefore inadequate health provision, among many other evils. It also appears to be changing the world's climate, with possibly catastrophic consequences for millions.

The Origin of Ideology

Basic to all ideologies is the assumption that if we can develop a science of human history, all religious belief becomes redundant. The age of ideology began with the movement of ideas known as the 'Enlightenment' in the eighteenth century. Fundamental to it was the belief that science would ultimately explain everything, and that the technologies and wisdoms based upon it would create a perfect society. The notion of original sin, which argues that we humans are radically flawed, was dismissed as merely a stratagem to enable clergies to retain control of society. The modern era that the 'Enlightenment' began was founded upon the notion that we humans need only see the future clearly in order to create it perfectly. We are only now beginning radically to question this assumption—but it remains the bedrock of public debate.

So there remains a deeply rooted void between the religious view of life—in which we humans as flawed creatures look first to God for spiritual healing—and the secular world in which most of us live, based as it is upon the notion that a purely rational approach can solve all problems. Western intellectuals are still mostly emphatic rationalists, scathing in their contempt for a religious view of life. This rationalist view dominates the media, whose only core principle is to maintain the market that supports the media. So modern life is separated intellectually from the spiritual roots of the West's basic values, such as equality. And the persistent inequalities that defy our rationalism, right in the heart of our greatest cities, are plain for all to see. This tragic and incomprehensible chasm between intentions and realities sends millions into drug dependency, the root of much violent crime. Meanwhile another abyss has yawned—the proven corruption of some of an older generation of prominent politicians across Europe, who sought personal and party financial support from the wealthy classes in their respective countries during the Cold War years. Idly we wonder which of today's politicians will be exposed in a decade's time for today's invisible misdeeds.

And yet another chasm exists between the TV fantasy world of advertising and the environmental decay that rampant consumerism necessarily causes. The sleek vehicles speeding across deserts or verdant countryside on the screen are actually the source of most urban atmospheric pollution, sucked in for our asthmatic children to breathe as they travel slowly to and from school in a city wilderness. The ideology of the free market is adapting with glacial slowness to the realisation that we cannot treat the thin layer of habitability that circles the globe as though it is indestructible.

Another void yawns in the integrity of politics. Market research is used to determine the marketability of political ideas, so leadership has become followership. Election manifestos are designed by marketing experts, the 'spin doctors'. Too seldom do our leaders raise difficult issues involving difficult choices (e.g. between rampant consumer technology and a healthy environment). So we are condemned to changing direction through disaster and crisis—even though these are now easily predictable.

Chasms in the Church

Our churches too are not always models of integrity. My own church manifests a chasm—between the wisdom locked up in church documents, and the lives we Catholics generally live. The Pope addresses the world from a Renaissance palace, condemning theological and pastoral experiments aimed at making Christianity relevant to the teaming millions of the third world. In Latin America and the West generally many senior clerics promoted by Rome seem committed to an introverted spiritual life which ignores the beatitudes—Jesus' passionate recognition of those at the base of the social pyramid. A real hunger for justice often seems lacking.

Christian fundamentalism also fails by implying that a sense of personal guilt—mainly about sexual sin—will drive us back to our Christian roots. It rejects every science that questions its literalist interpretation of the bible. So it uses the media to propagate a childish and contemptible caricature of Christianity which merely justifies the reciprocal contempt of sceptical intellectuals.

So there is a vast chasm also in our western culture between our Christian roots and our secular and rationalist world view. The natural mindset of our culture excludes a religious dimension, and those who still practise a religious faith have difficulty living it in a world that finds religious belief archaic and even ridiculous.

Inevitably this division is reflected within the mainstream Christian churches also. There is no broad consensus over the fundamental meaning of the Christ event, or over its implications for Christian life or modern society. At one extreme are the fundamentalists, at the other a tendency to read the bible as fiction, with no clear message for the modern world. Within the Catholic church, this tension between 'conservatives' and 'liberals' is particularly marked. The latter tend to value intellectual and spiritual freedom, and to see the church as an evolving institution, while the former tend to regard the church as an essentially unchangeable entity in which theological uniformity and clerical monopoly must reign supreme.

Individualism — Triumph and Tragedy

The past two centuries might justly be described as the Age of the Individual. Classical liberalism set out to liberate the individual from constraining social, political and religious subordination so that talents could be developed freely, with benefit to all. In many ways this faith has been justified. The brilliance of scientists from Newton to Einstein has revolutionised our understanding of the universe, while the practical genius of people such as Edison and Ford has revolutionised the material context of our lives. The novel, the art form based upon the drama and predicaments of the individual, became dominant in literature, enriching our perception of individual capabilities and perspectives. Often those novels became the foundation of a new art form, cinema, also focused usually upon the drama of individual lives, and therefore itself a creator of 'star' actors. Youth culture focuses upon gifted individuals also, their talents harnessed by modern reproductive sound technology and broadcast to a global audience. Still today brilliant minds in the field of microelectronics and computer software are changing the way in which our economies work, making themselves rich beyond the dreams of the ancient world.

Yet tragedy lies just below the surface. The brilliant success of a minority of gifted individuals often paradoxically destroys them by isolating them in a media goldfish bowl, and by providing them with opportunities for self-indulgence that undermine their relationships and their physical health. The climb to fame and fortune provides the discipline everyone needs—but once the peak is scaled what is there left to do with life? Too often this question is answered with excesses that the media are equally ready to publicise.

And what of those—the vast majority—who get nowhere near the summit they have set out to climb, and who therefore fail in their own estimation? The existence of a global culture means that human ambition scales itself upward also, guaranteeing that failure will be equally spectacular and more frequent.

Another consequence of rampant individualism is that family and community suffer. Individualism often becomes mere egotism and narcissism—the desire above all to be recognised—so that community's need for lives of quiet service is increasingly unfulfilled. Paradoxically, this then threatens us as individuals, because a society of narcissistic individuals is one in which self-concern is the only concern that can exist.

Individualism thus causes often another chasm, in our personal relationships. Here too promises are made, and then casually broken, with catastrophic consequences, particularly for children. The loss of a sense of eternal values and relationships has eroded our capacity to make secure lifetime commitments to one another. Partnerships become provisional, unable to withstand serious challenge or temptation.

Another void exists between what we consider to be our rights, and what we are prepared to contribute to the community that must deliver these rights. As community perishes, we are burdened as individuals with the consequences of our own selfishness—the random violence that is increasingly the recreation of an alienated youth culture. There comes a point, and we have reached it in the hearts of our greatest cities, where talk of rights becomes an irrational demand addressed to a void. Individualism threatens the individual just as dangerously as the collectivism of the past.

The Global Chasm between rich and poor

While the first world spends billions on weight reduction, millions of children die in the third world for lack of basic food and medicine. Our media cannot protect us from these realities either, but the problem persists. An estimated 200 million children around the globe are commercially exploited in tying tiny knots in carpets, making bricks, or fulfilling the sexual fantasies of middle aged entrepreneurs from the wealthier economies. Meanwhile our leaders focus on other priorities, telling us that their political careers rest upon our approval of this ideological selfishness. Our dreams are therefore filled with the horror of the avoidable sufferings of children, while we generally over-consume. This chasm—between the 'New World Order' promised after the fall of communism, and the situation a decade later—is perhaps the most glaring of all at the turn of the century.

The Crisis summarised

To summarise our condition briefly, we humans are now mostly deprived of faith and burdened by cynicism. Three hundred years ago we were told that Christianity was pernicious nonsense, and we began to invest heavily in an exclusive secularism. The churches helped in this process by attempting, in vain, to retain clerical control of thought—sometimes even to the extent of opposing perfectly Christian ideals espoused by secularists, such as social equality. Secularism—a view of life which excludes religious belief—has brought unquestionable prosperity to many and changed the world forever. However, secularism cannot explain or cure the spiritual desolation in which our civilisation now finds itself, with the evidence of human moral inertia plain for all to see. Sold the notion that there is no such thing as sin, we are now at a loss to explain, and to deal with, the phenomena that term once described. Our sceptical intelligentsia, once certain that God was dead, now tell us that certainty is unattainable. Reason taught us to abandon religious faith, and then deprived us of faith even in reason.

Thus, moral and cultural chasms abound at the end of the twentieth century. However, in an important sense, as Dennis Potter noticed, there is only one chasm—between the word and the deed, the intention and its realisation—in the secular and religious domains and within every one of us. This global chasm, caused simply by human selfishness, dominates the transition from the second to the third millennium. It deepens into a gathering crisis, out of which a different world must emerge if we are to survive. This cannot happen unless we are somehow released as individuals from the prison of our own self-absorption.

CHAPTER II

The Upward Journey and the Pyramid of Esteem

The chasm between the word and the deed is a pervasive phenomenon, affecting humans everywhere and throughout history. Yet today we in the West generally behave most of the time as though it doesn't exist, as though just one more rationalist theory will automatically move our species towards real happiness and fulfilment. Usually there is a jargon that goes with this new theory, a new terminology to accompany new ideals. For example, 'communitarianism', arising out of a perception that community is generally under threat, proposes that 'commitment' and 'solidarity' will make everything right. And so of course they would—if we had genuine commitment and solidarity, and a genuine sense of community. But the chasm still yawns between the intention and the reality, and the community still falls into it. And the existence of the chasm—the reality that characterises our human world more clearly than any other—remains unacknowledged.

The original reason for this is that the 'Enlightenment' made it a matter of dogmatic faith that no such chasm exists. The chasm—known for most of western history as sin—was the special province of the clergy, those obscurantist reactionaries who wished to shut out the light of reason, which would make everything right. Their specific expertise, knowledge of God and of good and evil, was believed to be obsolete, and their dominance of society was therefore seen as pernicious. Reason, not faith, would discover the truth about human behaviour, and once understood, this truth would free humankind from the superstition of sin.

Yet the chasm is not an intellectual problem. It can be discerned intellectually, but not closed intellectually—because it has to do not with thought but with action or, more often, inaction. The chasm is a moral problem, so that not even a perfect and omniscient psychology will solve it. To illustrate, think of yourself at your most indolent. Is there a theory that will automatically solve this problem?

There is, of course, another reason why 'sin' is an awkward term in the late twentieth century. Christian fundamentalists tend to apply it predominantly to a specific area of human failure—sexual error—and to ignore its application to others (for example the 'covetousness' or greed upon which our over-consuming culture is based). As a result, the term tends to be associated with people who are hung up on sexual evil, which is why I have approached it in terms of a mysterious but pervasive tendency of us humans to live in non-conformity with our own highest aspirations, affecting all aspects of our lives, including the sexual. It is also therefore an inability to live happily, to bridge the gulf between our highest hopes and our best achievements.

It is also true that enormous benefits flowed from the secularisation of western society, and from the elevation of science to a dominant role in education. We have had two centuries of extraordinary progress in our technical control of the material problems of life. We have also developed to an extraordinary degree the range of occupations available to children on the brink of life, increasing the possibility that developed talents will be matched with career niches. These are the great benefits of modern life—but the chasm still intrudes. We are developing an underclass of people whose talents are undeveloped and who can find no niche, and their despair is a reproach and a threat to the rest of us. In one critically important respect human society has not changed at all: wealth and power is skewed in favour of a minority, and there remains even in the most advanced economies a deprived third, the disadvantaged who cannot rise up the meritocratic ladder.

After two centuries of ideological attempts to resolve this problem, we should be ready to acknowledge that ideologies as such are counter-egalitarian. They are created and then fully understood only by intellectuals who demand the privileges to which their expertise entitles them. So the Soviet Union, supposedly founded upon the pure idealism of Karl Marx, was in fact based upon a communist party elite given privileged and exclusive access to the consumer goods of the West. Anyone who publicly noticed this flagrant disregard for the egalitarian principles of Marx was consigned to the Gulags. This was the moral chasm which eventually undermined the system completely. It proved the tenacity of human selfishness, and the common tendency of our species throughout history to build pyramids of power and esteem which are unjust.

Yet the pyramid of respect and power is just as pervasive in the West. Based upon the free market, our economies concentrate wealth and power in the hands of those who control and develop technology. The classic example is Bill Gates, CEO of the most successful computer software firm on earth. His personal fortune in 1998 was estimated at over $50 billion. Yet median income in the USA was no higher in that year than it had been in 1989, although longer hours were being worked to maintain that income. Poverty levels had not changed in the same decade. Thirty million people, including 13 million children, suffered from involuntary hunger in the richest economy on earth.

Why do we maintain these pyramids, despite such a long historical experience of their injustice? Why are they so tenacious? The answer appears to be that nearly all of us see our lives as an upward journey to success, which we define as the recognition and admiration of the world. And this has always been the case. True, there are many differences between the life of Bill Gates and that of Marcus Licinius Crassus, but both aimed at amazing the world, and both succeeded—and their worlds were both dominated by an elite that ignored the deprivation that surrounded them.

Gates' story is well known. In the early 1980s he dropped out of university to develop the basic software that gave IBM's newly designed microcomputer, the PC, its ability to interact with its first users. Using this knowledge, Gates and his firm Microsoft set out to develop the other software—word processors, spreadsheets, databases—that the mass-market PC owner would use. By the late 1990s Microsoft had a virtual monopoly in these fields, while the PC had become the standard microcomputer in business and the home, with an estimated 600 million in use worldwide. Gates dominated the most dynamic industry on earth, and was fighting to maintain his virtual software monopoly against antitrust moves by his rivals. These had gained some leverage with the US government due to Gates' commercial bid to dominate the Internet software market also.

It is clear enough that Gates is one of the most gifted entrepreneurs on earth, and a model for thousands who seek to follow him. They seem completely fulfilled in their successful scaling of the pyramid, that upward journey towards wealth and public acclaim, and their commercial success guarantees the durability of the pyramid itself. Their aim is to become one of those fifty 'movers and shakers' lauded annually in *Time* magazine—for it is the function of the media also to concentrate the attention of the world on the successful minority—to maintain the world's belief that some people are vastly more important than others. We consumers of the media then do our bit to help to maintain the pyramid by buying into this admiration of the few. It is axiomatic that only a few people can be really important, so that most humans must be ignored and frustrated. Apparently, that is the way we want the world to be. We buy the media output that consigns us to the role of spectator of the lives of others, convinced that we ourselves are unimportant.

The Roman world in 70 BC knew nothing of microcomputers, but just as much as we do about the adulation of the few. Their word for adulation was glory, possessed only by Gods and great men who just might become Gods themselves. In that year, Marcus Licinius Crassus took a further step on his upward journey by ordering the crucifixion of 6,000 rebellious slaves along the Appian Way from Padua to Rome. Slaves provided the home comforts of much of the Roman elite, so the possibility of a slave revolt necessarily haunted their dreams. This mass execution served two purposes—to terrify all slaves into mute obedience, and to further Crassus' political career. The upward journey must necessarily have a dual result: the advancement of 'great men' and the subordination of others who, at this extreme, become naked victims whom history will necessarily forget.

The essential point here is the connection between the upward journey and the social pyramid. One confirms and supports the other. At the summit of the pyramid of esteem there will always be a small minority of powerful people, at the base a horde of nonentities, some of whom will become victims.

Throughout human history, from the ancient world to the world of the microchip, this is an essential element of continuity. Because of human selfishness, power and recognition is concentrated in an elite who then dominate a social system which must deny both to a majority. The upward journey, the heroic journey of the ancient world and the commercial world still today, creates the pyramid which in turn condemns the majority to obscurity, self-disregard and sometimes extreme suffering. Here we find the origin of all chasms also, in all historical periods. The prevalence of the upward journey, celebrated in almost all literature, bears witness to a human fixation with recognising and rewarding the few at the expense of the many. Money now substitutes for the honours and titles of the past, commercial competition for military rivalry, but the essential result is the same—the pyramid of esteem which condemns most of us to self-dislike.

It is only when we see this pattern as a human constant that we can begin to understand the historical person who was Jesus, for his journey, far more emphatically than any other in human history, was in precisely the opposite direction—not upward towards glory or apotheosis like that of Augustus and Tiberius (his contemporaries), but downward towards recognition of the powerless, personal execration and violent death, in precisely the mode chosen by Crassus to humiliate the slaves. We may remember that Spartacus was the leader of those whom Crassus immolated, but the rest are nameless. So should be all the crucified victims of Pontius Pilate. Yet this was the destination that Jesus chose.

Even if we are determined to exclude the possibility of Jesus' divinity, we for that very reason are faced with a profound mystery. Why would anyone, particularly anyone so gifted, choose this impossible journey towards ultimate pain and humiliation?

CHAPTER III

The Impossible Journey

All of the heroes of the ancient world, real or mythical, embarked upon the upward journey. Theseus' journey was from Troezen to Athens to win the recognition of his father Aegeus. On the way he slew three monsters who waylaid travellers. This sequence is important: first the hero must achieve glory through heroic violence, then he is recognised. Aegeus' recognition is followed by that of Athens itself when Theseus slays the Minotaur on Crete. He inherits the kingdom.

So the journey to Athens is also an upward journey to recognition and glory, ultimately the recognition of the Gods themselves. It is axiomatic that this recognition is denied until the upward journey is accomplished. It follows that those who make no heroic journey remain unrecognised by men or Gods, and lead lives of no importance.

This was the Greek tradition, but the Roman was based upon it, and identical in this respect. So, gifted individuals whose historical existence is certain embarked upon the same journey. Alexander's military campaigns in Asia, the most extraordinary of the ancient world, brought him unparalleled adulation, so much so that Julius Caesar later wept at the thought that he could never excel them. Yet Caesar set out anyway on the upward journey that led him to conquest in Gaul, assassination in Rome and then recognition as a God by his protégé Octavian, later Augustus. These upward journeys, among others, transformed Rome from a republic into the most expansive empire the world had yet seen.

Even Jewish culture extolled the upward journey. Its greatest hero, David, sprang to prominence by challenging and slaying the giant philistine, Goliath. Yet Jewish culture also had a strange addiction to the truth, expressed through the prophets. Nathan the prophet did not scruple to broadcast the truth of how David acquired Bathsheba, by using his royal prerogative to have her husband Uriah placed in the thick of battle where he would be certain to die. David, to his credit, did not deny Nathan's accusation or punish his temerity—but most of the prophets were not so lucky. The Jewish people were unique in this tradition of prophetic criticism of their own flaws—another mysterious phenomenon. What was the satisfaction in being a prophet if you typically got killed for it? Yet the prophetic tradition survived, Israel's real glory.

David is important, because the expected Messiah was modelled on David in the Jewish imagination. It followed that the Messiah must emerge as a military hero and recover exclusive possession of Israel, expelling the power of Rome. It did not occur to them that a journey that was to excel that of David might be also a prophetic journey, downward to tragedy.

The Journey Begins

From the start of the narrative in Luke we are warned that Jesus is set upon an unprecedented and contradictory journey. The *Magnificat* tells us that in the incarnation God has 'used the power of his arm' and 'routed the arrogant of heart'. 'He has pulled down princes from their thrones and raised high the lowly.' (Lk 1:51, 52)

Straightaway it is clear that Jesus is not to be another David, for princes as such are to be pulled down, and the lowly raised. The world—the pyramid of esteem, envy and abuse of power—is to be challenged, and a completely new order set in train.

His journey begins at the river Jordan, with John the Baptist. John's baptism in these waters, symbolic of freedom and renewal, implies that God's favour can be won by simple repentance, and is therefore a challenge to the Temple system, the summit of the religious upward journey. Thus it is the best place for Jesus to begin the downward journey.

From where did he get the psychological and spiritual strength for this journey, which will end in hell itself? The gospel record suggests that it came directly from the Father. 'As he was coming up out of the water, he saw the heavens torn apart and the Spirit like a dove descending on him. And a voice came from heaven, 'You are my son, the beloved; my favour rests on you'.' (Mk 1: 10, 11)

This episode reverses the normal sequence of events on the upward journey: first we achieve, then we are recognised and affirmed. Jesus has received a most extraordinary recognition—the love and respect of the Creator—even before he begins his mission. Whether or not this recognition was noticed by anyone else is not important. Jesus experiences the overwhelming love of Jahweh. As this world has nothing greater to offer, he can resist the temptations to follow.

Jesus' sojourn in the desert

The desert is a place of profound isolation, peace and silence. It is therefore the place to go to commune with the discovered God, who is so utterly different from the world. It is the place in which Jesus, in communion with the Father, comes to an understanding of that world, and of the upward journey to human acclaim which tempts all of us, and which would separate him from the Father. We are told that here he faced three temptations, (Mt 4:1-11). The first is to turn stone into bread, using the divine favour he has received to resolve his immediate physical need. He rejects it because he is at the same time hearing still the words he heard at the Jordan, 'You are my son, the beloved'—words from the mouth of God. As this hunger for divine recognition is greater than any physical hunger, he is satisfied in his own deepest being, and finds the physical hunger secondary and trivial. The primacy of the spiritual life, in communion with the Father, is thus affirmed. Frequently thereafter he walks apart in communion with the Father.

The second temptation is to amaze the religious elite who control the Temple system, by throwing himself from its parapet into the arms of God. If he is raised up by God in the eyes of all who dominate the system, is this not the quickest route to spiritual glory? This temptation is greater than the first, but this too he rejects. Since he has the Father's favour, the acclaim of the spiritual leadership of Israel is not compelling—he does not need to climb that pyramid either, even by the fastest route.

The third is the temptation to political power, most tempting of all to a Jew who resented the captivity of his people by the blasphemous Romans and their Herodian collaborators. Yet this too he rejects. Somehow he has grown so close to the Father that the temptation of worldly power has no irresistible force. The political pyramid is not for scaling either. He is to be heroic in a sense that David and Alexander could not have understood.

The Journey of Recognition

Grounded in the love of the Father, Jesus does not need to ascend either the religious or the political pyramids. And, loving the Father, he learns of the Father's overwhelming concern for those who cannot ascend, those at the base of both pyramids. He has discovered that no-one is unloved, and that there is nothing we have still to do to merit that love, and this discovery he must share with those who will be most joyful on learning it. Those to whom that truth can be communicated will experience the kingdom of God.

Thus Jesus seeks the company of the rejected. He declares that the kingdom of God belongs to the poor, or the poor in spirit. He freely breaches the minutiae of the law. He heals the sick and the demonically possessed. He assaults the dignity of the religious elites. In this phase of his mission he sets out to include in God's love all those who saw themselves as undeserving of it—even the Gentiles who came in faith. Far from seeking recognition from the elites, he is himself embarked on a journey through which the excluded are recognised and loved.

It is a measure of the success of the churches so far that we today do not identify God's favour with the favour of the world, that we recognise that God loves the poor. The apostles did not know that initially. 'How then can anyone be saved?' they ask Jesus, when the latter has lamented the difficulty the rich will have in entering the kingdom of heaven. (Lk 18:26) It is important to pause a moment to explain this.

For most Jews of Jesus' time, poverty, mental illness and physical diseases of all kinds were associated with God's disfavour. Tragic accidents were also believed to be evidence of sin. The 613 laws of Leviticus placed a minutely complicated barrier between the individual and God's forgiveness, and negotiating this required the services of the scribes, religious lawyers. Only the purchase of these services—impossible for the poor—allowed the Temple expiation—another expense—which supposedly completed the process of winning divine favour. It followed that, for Peter, the well-to-do alone seemed blessed with divine favour.

This was the deepest source of the antagonism that Jesus encountered from most of the religious elite. He travelled about far from the Temple (mostly), proclaiming the forgiveness of sins to those who showed faith in him, undermining the Temple-centred religious system and the clerical apparatus that depended upon it. This was essentially a subversion of the influence of the religious elites.

It follows that in teaching the unmerited love of God, Jesus was on a collision course with those who believed in and relied upon the Temple system.

The End of Exclusion

It is not just individuals who form hierarchies and who embark upon upward journeys. Kinship groups or tribes, cities and nations may do so also. Judaism saw itself as embarked upon an upward journey with Jahweh as guide and protector. In this sense, God belonged to the Jews, and would vindicate them in the end. There was a hierarchy of nations, and it was the destiny of the chosen people to climb this pyramid. The Messiah was to be the one who would lead them in this journey.

Even John has evidently learned that the Father's love extends beyond the Jews, and so tells them that God does not belong to them, and could raise a people 'from these stones'. (Lk 3:8) Israel's glory was the fidelity of Jahweh, but now it is time to declare his love for all of humankind, without exclusion.

Jesus himself does not belong to his own kin either: 'whoever does the will of God is my brother and mother and sister' (Mk 3:35). To all who approach, whether prostitute, Jewish official, Roman officer or Syro-Phoenician woman, there is just one condition for his help—faith. But this inclusiveness too is a source of scandal and opposition.

Jesus Accuses the Accusers

Typically the elites who dominate the religious pyramid are armed with rules. Mastery of such rules gives them the power they need to assert their own rank, and to bar the ascent of rivals. So it is with the scribes and Pharisees who challenge Jesus on such vital lapses as failure to wash hands and forearms before meals, chewing grain on the Sabbath, and sitting down with tax sharks. Such elites are usually blind to the truth that, by making so much of these things, they are declaring their God to be an elitist also. The Old Testament itself bore witness to the foolishness of this belief.

Jesus's response breaks all the rules of the normal ascending journey. Instead of flattering his accusers in the hope of their patronage, he is consistently critical. 'Hypocrites', 'vipers', 'whitewashed tombs', 'murderers of the prophets', 'worthy of hell'—his opponents are all of these things. (Mt 23)

It is clear that he is attacking, not individuals, but whole classes. It is the pyramid of exclusion itself that he is set upon toppling. This again is deadly dangerous, for such pyramids are always self-protective, to the point of violence.

The Kingdom of God

Jesus's rejection of the hierarchical tyrannies of the ancient world begs an obvious question: what should replace them? His answer is 'the kingdom of God', which will belong to the poor and poor in spirit, the just, the infirm, those innocent as children and those who make sacrifices for

Jesus's sake. Only the proud, and those who think they already belong, are in danger of being excluded from it. It is clearly a no-go zone for elites, because in it everyone is aware of being loved infinitely and equally.

Jesus' driving compassion for the excluded is most closely expressed in the Sermon on the Mount, (Mt 5, 6). He embodies the divine compassion, which is why he is loved by everyday people to whom life has taught humility. God's purpose is anti-hierarchical precisely because it is the hierarchies who have most economic and political power. Yet those who have acquired wealth and position will be the least generous and least flexible, because their self-respect is dependent upon what they already own, and what the world envies. The problem of the young man who could not abandon his fortune is the problem of elites everywhere and always, and of the West today: we have convinced ourselves that only in what we own lies our importance and our fulfilment. The kingdom of God is the opposite of this world.

Blessed are the poor. Again we need to remind ourselves how revolutionary this was for people who supposed their poverty to be the result of divine disfavour. Jesus is sharing the divine recognition he has received with people who supposed themselves hated by God. This news has always been remembered, through an oral rather than written tradition, wherever Christianity has travelled—a constant scourge to elites down the centuries.

The Challenge

Yet there is more than recognition of the poor in the Sermon on the Mount. There is also the challenge, particularly the challenge to forgiveness and love of the enemy. We resent that such a hard law should be imposed, but need to understand that, since it is presented from a position of powerlessness, challenge, not law, is in question. This 'word' is not an impossible burden imposed by a remote and intolerant deity, but an invitation to a new kind of heroism, from a vulnerable person who is prepared to live and die by the same values.

The Education of the Apostles

His chosen twelve disciples he meanwhile seeks to educate in the nature of the new order, the kingdom of God. He found it hard going.

> Jesus noticed how some of the guests were choosing the best places, so he told this parable to all of them: 'When someone invites you to a wedding feast, do not sit down in the best place. It could happen that someone more important than you has been invited, and your host, who invited both of you, would have to come and say to you, "Let him have this place." Then you would be embarrassed and have to sit in the lowest place. Instead, when you are invited, go and sit in the lowest place, so that your host will come to you and say, "Come on up, my friend, to a better place." This will bring you honour in the presence of all the other guests. For everyone who makes himself great will be humbled, and everyone who humbles himself will be made great.' (Lk 14:7-11)

But he is battling against millennia of social hierarchy.

> At that time the disciples came to Jesus, asking, 'Who is the greatest in the kingdom of heaven?' So Jesus called a child, made him stand in front of them, and said, 'I assure you that unless you change and become like children, you will never enter the kingdom of heaven. The greatest in the kingdom is the one who humbles himself and becomes like this child. And whoever welcomes in my name one such child as this, welcomes me.' (Mt 18:1-4)

'Who is the greatest?' Adult man at his most childish, and most envious. The child has not yet set out upon the upward journey, and is content with what respect he already enjoys. He (or she) is closer to the kingdom, closer to his real self, not yet rejecting himself in favour of a chosen, superior model.

> Then James and John, the sons of Zebedee, came to him. 'Teacher,' they said, 'we want you to do for us whatever we ask.' 'What do you want me to do for you?' he asked. They replied, 'Let one of us sit at your right and the other at your left in your glory.' (Mk 10:35, 36)

When they hear of it the other ten are annoyed, but on their own behalf. So Jesus needs to say:

> 'You know that those who are regarded as rulers of the Gentiles lord it over them, and their high officials exercise authority over them. Not so with you. Instead, whoever wants to become great among you must be your servant, and whoever wants to be first must be slave of all. For even the Son of Man did not come to be served, but to serve, and to give his life as a ransom for many.'(Mk 10:42-45)

In Luke's gospel the same thing happens at the last supper.

> A dispute arose also between them about which should be reckoned the greatest, but he said to them, 'Among pagans it is the king who lords it over them, and those who have authority over them are given the title Benefactor. This must not happen with you. No, the greatest among you must behave as though he were the youngest, the leader as though he were the one who serves. For who is the greater: the one at table or the one who serves? The one at table, surely, yet here am I among you as the one who serves!' (Lk 22:24-27)

Easily missed in these passages is a profoundly important truth: Jesus has not created among his followers a hierarchy of esteem. Had he done so, there would have been no dispute or doubt as to who was the greatest. His egalitarianism throws them into an anxious quarrel aimed at reestablishing hierarchy. This is the besetting sin of all elites. The sons of Zebedee still have in mind an upward journey and a pyramid of esteem.

It is in St John's gospel that we find the most pointed and moving lessons in the egalitarianism of the new order. First of all, in his altercation with his enemies, Jesus directly challenges the ancient world's conception of heroism:

> 'Human glory means nothing to me . . . How can you believe, since you look to each other for glory and are not concerned with the glory that comes from the one God.'
> (Jn 5:41, 44)

'You look to each other for glory.' This simple diagnosis of what is wrong with society in Jesus' time stands also as a valid criticism of, and for, all time. We compete with one another for the adulation of the world, as though that world consisted of beings who were not themselves involved in the same competition, as unsure as ourselves of what makes a human action 'glorious'. In Jesus time 'glory' was associated strongly with military prowess. With us it is associated mostly with an ability to make money, or with a flair for attracting publicity. In all cases, throughout history, we award it for arbitrary and ridiculous reasons. We want both to rise above our peers, and possess their esteem — an entirely irrational enterprise, since their resentment will fight against their admiration. This kind of glory is fickle and treacherous, but we seek it nevertheless.

Jesus' values are centred elsewhere, as we see in the following passage from the narrative of the last supper:

> Jesus knew that the father had given him complete power;
> he knew that he had come from God and was going to

God. So he rose from the table, took off his outer garment, and tied a towel round his waist. Then he poured some water into a basin and began to wash the disciples' feet and dry them with the towel round his waist. He came to Simon Peter, who said to him, 'Are you going to wash my feet, Lord?' Jesus said 'You do not understand now what I am doing, but you will understand later.' Peter declared, 'Never at any time will you wash my feet!' 'If I do not wash your feet,' Jesus answered, 'you will no longer be my disciple.' (Jn 13:3-8)

Two things should be noted in this passage. First, the apparent contradiction between the gift of complete power, and the action that follows. Jesus does not do what the upward journey requires at this point—outline a strategy for Jewish emancipation from Roman power—but something entirely baffling to his followers, the performance of a menial task. The power of God is expressed in service, not domination. There is no more extraordinary passage in the Gospels.

Secondly, why is this lesson acted out? Because of the potency of lived example. Since Jesus is the model of the new order, his followers must witness service and self-abasement in him. This passage is a summary of the downward journey that Jesus is embarked upon. It also emphasises the difficulty of convincing the leaders of his community of the need for a downward journey within themselves. It is therefore a premonition also of the possibility that in the absence of the model even Jesus' closest followers will revert to type. The ambivalent history of the Christian clergy, including the papacy—verbose witnesses to a downward journey they themselves would often reverse and contradict—is thus prefigured, in particular the ambivalence of Peter.

Peter Doesn't Get It
It is striking that Peter, throughout the story, expects to see Jesus emerge as another David, recreating the normal hierarchy, and assuming leadership of

it. When Jesus first broaches the prospect of death for himself in Jerusalem, Peter takes him aside and remonstrates. (Mt 16:21-23) The removal of Jesus from the group for this purpose is Peter's way of establishing the conventional hierarchy. Jesus must not be rebutted publicly, for this would diminish him. He must be taken aside and reproached by his first officer. Peter's objective is to persuade Jesus that he can succeed as David did, emerge as the hero of his people — and then reward his closest supporters, Peter uppermost.

Jesus, however, sees Peter's appeal as Satanic, because it tempts him again to the upward journey, the temptation last offered by Satan in the desert.

Peter's opposition to the foot-washing shows he has still not understood. If Jesus washes his feet, how can he, Peter, expect deference from those who will become his subordinates in the new order? Will he be expected to wash their feet? This would turn the world upside down!

But this is exactly what Jesus is about. 'You do not understand now what I am doing, but you will understand later.' (Jn 13:7) Two millennia later Peter still doesn't quite get it. Hierarchy is extraordinarily tenacious.

Where does this power come from? Probably simply from the fact that each of us grows within a hierarchical system which precedes us. We observe the pyramids of esteem within which we find ourselves, and school ourselves to find a position within the hierarchy from which we can begin our own ascent. Our self-evaluation depends upon others' evaluation of ourselves. The question from above that we dread is 'Just who the hell do you think you are?' The invitation we hope for is one that comes also from above. 'We are delighted to tell you that you have received promotion to branch manager!' The lives of billions are now lived stressfully between this fear and this hope, with most unsure of whether they should be unmasked or promoted. This is the penalty we all pay for the upward journey, the search for recognition in other humans who are also mostly on the same search, and therefore fundamentally indifferent to us, or even hostile and unpredictable.

For Peter before the Resurrection, the fear of rejection by the world was greater than the love of Christ. His final gesture to prevent disaster—the use of a sword at Gethsemane—was designed to rescue Jesus from total failure, as David had rescued Saul from Goliath. Frustrated, he then watched the process by which Jesus was finally brought to account, and could not find the strength to identify and stand with him.

Before Pilate, Jesus does not claim the sovereignty that Pilate uses to condemn him, saying only that his kingdom 'is not of this world'. (Jn 18: 36) Pilate does not see this as a threat to Roman power, but bows to the pressure of the moment, the demand for crucifixion. Jesus accepts this without reproach, and asks for forgiveness for those who now crucify him.

Two questions are raised by this unique and terrible journey. First, what exactly could be its purpose? Second, from where came the inspiration and strength needed to conceive and carry through such a life, to such a bitter end—the antithesis of glory?

CHAPTER IV

The Kingdom

The purpose of the downward journey is, first, to subvert the pyramid of esteem by showing solidarity not with those who maintain it, but with those who suffer from it. That pyramid is the product of all the selfishness in society, the desire to ascend, so it is this selfishness that is challenged by the downward journey. In this sense, when we pursue thoughtlessly the upward journey, no matter what rank we occupy, without considering those at the base of the pyramid of esteem, we are complicit in their subordination. So the crucifixion challenges us all.

Yet there is even more in this event. The upward journey skews wealth and power towards a minority, disempowering and impoverishing and always disappointing a majority. It follows that most are deprived of freedom, self-esteem and economic security. This is less true today than in the ancient world, but still largely true even in the wealthiest societies. Political freedom is no substitute for freedom from hunger and self-contempt.

It follows that the deliberate downward journey is intended to bring the gift of self-esteem to all, by changing the direction of human ambition from ascent, accumulation, self-empowerment, to service of and concern for the disadvantaged. A man who chooses to make this journey, and travels it to its terrifying conclusion, has issued a challenge to all men, particularly to those who doubt his divinity. For if he wasn't God he was a 'mere' man relying upon purely natural human resources. For all of us, no matter what our faith, race, or level of education, this journey becomes a challenge, once we understand it.

The Kingdom Revealed

What would happen to human culture if many began the downward journey? From the life of Jesus we get glimpses of this, and from many of the lives of the saints.

First, and most important, the pyramid of esteem is upended. All people are esteemed, particularly those who tolerate poverty without complaint. This is what Jesus meant when he said 'blessed are the poor in spirit'. When in 1208 CE, Francis donned his coarse habit tied with a rope he stepped into the kingdom of God, dignifying poverty and simplicity. This was an outstanding intuition of the downward journey that helped to redeem his era, which was also the era of the Inquisition. Throughout its ambivalent history, the church can point to such people as exemplars of the life of Christ, even though at its summit the church provided often a contrary example.

Secondly, conflict is no more, for it is the upward journey that pits people against one another in envy and jealousy. When esteem is the monopoly of a minority, most people must fail to acquire it, and this is a formula for resentment and violent crime. And it is the upward journey of states that for the same reason leads to oppression and international conflict.

Thirdly, psychological problems related to the upward journey are undercut. For example, the belief that only certain rare physiological characteristics can be described as sexually attractive is the basis of the 'beauty' pyramid maintained by the media on behalf of the entertainment, cosmetics and fashion industries. It is also the source of much adolescent self-hatred, self-starvation and addiction. The beauty pyramid is just another pyramid of esteem that destroys people. Variety of appearance should be seen as the necessary basis of individuality, not an undesirable deviation from an arbitrary norm. In the kingdom, all are beautiful, because they are different. This example can be replicated in all other social pyramids.

Fourthly, whereas in the world only a small minority are recognised, in the kingdom everyone receives the recognition of the Father, as Jesus did at the Jordan, but through those already in the kingdom. For each of us has been made by him with loving care, over aeons of time. This recognition can be communicated by loving Christian communities treating all their members, and all they meet, with equal respect.

Fifthly, a world that condemns most of its citizens to failure in their own estimation can become a kingdom in which all succeed by the development of their own talents, equally esteemed.

Finally, we can be ourselves, rather than the persons we believe the world wants us to be. To pursue this we need to understand the idea of repentance.

Repentance

This term has always had doubtful connotations. Christian fundamentalism tends to portray repentance simply as the acknowledgement of guilt, an abject kneeling and self-accusation, an acknowledgement of one's own moral failures before a perfect God, a surrender of self-respect and freedom. And 'conversion' tends to mean surrender also, the rejection of the self, a submission and capitulation, an acknowledgement that God has won our soul and we have lost our freedom.

The reality is different. It involves a recognition of God, a realisation that he is not what or whom we thought. And a rediscovery of the self.

From adolescence we humans unconsciously try to be the person we admire, not the very different person we were intended to be. This is especially true because of the pyramid of esteem — we esteem ourselves less than those we perceive to be above us in the pyramid, and so set out to suppress the unesteemed self in favour of those others we envy. So we become dependent upon others for our self-respect, which makes us very vulnerable to rejection. The problem is that those others are usually playing the same game, and are therefore also alienated from themselves, and unable to give us the recognition we desire. The child who meets contempt from other children, or from an adult, will often suppose she deserves it, and may then try to suppress whatever behaviour or mannerism they sneer at. An accumulation of such attempts becomes the personality she shows the world.

This process can be called the wearing of masks—the gradual and unconscious substitution of an altered personality for the real personality in order to achieve recognition, or to deflect contempt. True repentance involves a realisation that we do not have to do that any more. For there is nothing we can do to earn the love of God. That love is implicit in our creation. God loves us from the beginning, and will always do so. It is the world, the pyramid of esteem, not God, who deprives us of that knowledge. And it is part of the purpose of Jesus' downward journey to give us the strength to pull away the mask—that which conceals our real self. For the thing that separates us most from God is self-dislike, and God has gone to great lengths to deprive us of that. To understand this we need to understand another aspect of the cross.

Humiliation and The Cross

Let us suppose that we want to humiliate someone—to destroy totally any respect anyone may ever have felt for them, before killing them. We want to destroy the soul, the sense of self-worth, before destroying the body. That was the cross. The victim was stripped entirely naked, nailed or bound to this gibbet and then raised aloft so that all could sneer and jeer. To the agony of physical pain was added the agony of total shame and humiliation, and days could pass in this double suffering. At the base of the pyramid of esteem, people are stripped completely of self-regard as well as life.

And this is why those at the bottom of the pyramid may suddenly, seeing the cross, break down and weep. At a level much deeper than the conscious mind, they suddenly experience the meaning of the crucifixion. It is the living God joining them on their cross. It is the solidarity of the Father with the least of his creation. It is his acceptance of humiliation as a means of making contact with theirs. In this realisation also, atonement occurs, for our search for a person without flaw is over. He lives, and he loves us for who we are.

And so we are also released from the mask. For since we are loved so totally for our real self, there is no need ever again to try to be someone else. And then we realise that the Father is not what we thought he was—that aloof judge who records our every fault. He has instead felt every slight we have ever suffered, and joined us in that pain. And then we feel for him, and weep. And he responds with what the saints call grace, and we weep uncontrollably for ever having doubted him. We may often do so again thereafter, for there is no complete recovery from this moment.

And in this process there is also the rediscovery of the child we once were, before we set out upon the upward journey. For we realise that we do not ever again need to compare ourselves unfavourably with others, that we can be our true innocent selves. We can be as children again. This is repentance.

Conversion

When we discover God and ourselves in the process of repentance, love of God will follow. If we allow it to, this love will change our lives completely. We rediscover the Christian ethic as something designed to set us free, not to deny us happiness. This change is called conversion.

The discovery of God changes everything. We do not need to be afraid. We are no longer trapped by the pyramid of esteem because we are no longer dependent upon the approval of others for self-approval. And we are no longer locked in conflict with those around us, for we know the upward journey is futile and unnecessary. The realisation of the inalienable love of God is a rock-solid foundation for self-esteem, and we long to share this realisation with others.

In particular, we long to share the knowledge that there is no such thing as a failed, or ruined, life. We have discovered that the moment of deepest despair is also the most likely moment for the discovery of God, and are gripped by the desire to pass that realisation on to those we love, at the precise moment this message becomes a matter of life and death.

There is even more in the downward journey, however. At the base of the pyramid of esteem is the victim, the person from whom everything is stripped, including life itself. The crucifixion of the 6,000 by Crassus was an attempt to re-stabilise the Roman Empire through ultimate violence. There is a compelling argument that another purpose of Jesus' journey was to expose the role of this 'scapegoating' violence in founding culture.

CHAPTER V

The Crucifixion and the Key of Knowledge

Although contemporary secular intellectuals are generally sceptical about Christianity and the notion of divine inspiration of the bible, cultural anthropologists associated with the academic René Girard are quite convinced that the biblical record is, after all, of a different order from all other ancient texts, and entirely capable of throwing new light on the predicament in which we now find ourselves.

For Girard, we humans are primarily mimetic creatures, that is to say we learn and grow by imitation at an unconscious level. Children imitate their parents intuitively, simply as a means of learning as rapidly as possible. There is no problem with this until someone takes or 'appropriates' something—the child a toy, or the man a tool, say. 'Mimetic' desire then dictates that there will often be an imitative act of appropriation by someone else of the same object—and conflict may begin. And when one blow is struck, mimesis also dictates that others may follow. In a society dissolving in mimetic conflict, there is a growing irrationality and terror. A mechanism is required which will break the cycle of mimetic violence, for otherwise all will perish.

This mechanism is the accusation of an individual in some way isolated from the rest, e.g. by the fact that he or she is a stranger, or disfigured. This individual's isolation means that his death will not provoke the reciprocal vengeance of any sizeable faction. So he is accused of being somehow the source of the evil that now afflicts his society, and either put to death by the entire community, or expelled. Reciprocal violence threatening to destroy a society is thus replaced by a focused violence which reunites the same society around the body of an expendable individual. One person dies to 'save' the rest.

However, the unity thus created is precarious because of its origins in murder. So there begins a process of concealment of the truth in a founding myth, supported by a commemorative sacrificial ritual. A familiar example is the Oedipus legend, the story of the lamed stranger found to be the source of the plague affecting Thebes, and then blinded and driven out. Oedipus is at once the source of the plague (a metaphor for the crisis of mimetic violence), and the foundational figure of the religion designed to maintain the unity of the city. A regular ritual sacrifice replaces the original violent event. At some stage the victim typically becomes a God — far too late to enjoy the experience. Girard believes that all religions and foundation myths can be deconstructed to reveal the original scapegoating event, and provides many examples.[1]

For Girard, however, the biblical texts are unique in one vital respect. From first to last they introduce a moral dimension, an ongoing and overt critique of the scapegoating process, a refusal to conceal it by distorting the essential innocence of the scapegoat. Abel's blood 'cries out from the ground' to accuse Cain (Gen 4:10), where (in the Roman equivalent) Remus is accused of provoking Romulus' attack upon him. The prophets consistently reveal the evil of scapegoating violence, and themselves fall victim to it. This makes them unique in the history of ancient cultures, in which intellectuals generally complied in mythologising murder into heroic defence of the culture against monstrousness. Where the legend of Oedipus insists that he had murdered his father and committed incest with his mother, the story of Joseph (Gen 37) reveals the latter to have been victimised by his brothers out of jealousy. In the bible, uniquely and consistently, the victim's innocence is emphasised rather than concealed.

In the Old Testament this exposé of the scapegoating process reaches its greatest intensity in Isaiah's suffering servant.

> For he grew up before him like a young plant,
> and like a root out of dry ground;
> he had no form or comeliness that we should look at him,
> and no beauty that we should desire him.
> He was despised and rejected by men;
> a man of sorrows, and acquainted with grief;
> and as one from whom men hide their faces
> he was despised, and we esteemed him not. (Is 53:2-3)

The passage describes someone who is the antithesis of the typical hero of the ancient world—someone like Hercules who has divine connections and great physical strength and beauty. This therefore is someone who lacks esteem, someone in fact rejected, which means that his death will not provoke retaliation. He is the ideal scapegoat.

> By oppression and judgement he was taken away;
> and as for his generation, who considered
> that he was cut off from out of the land of the living,
> stricken for the transgression of my people?
> And they made his grave with the wicked
> and with a rich man in his death,
> although he had done no violence,
> and there was no deceit in his mouth. (Is 53:8-9)

Here again the text explicitly denies that any significant charge can be laid against the victim—his only crimes are pacifism and honesty, the specific virtues his accusers lack, for they will both lie about him and kill him.

Direct Accusation before the Event

In the gospels of both Matthew and Luke, there comes a moment when Jesus recapitulates the Old Testament, for the benefit of those who will soon turn upon him for precisely the same reasons.

> Therefore I send you prophets and wise men and scribes, some of whom you will kill and crucify, and some you will scourge in your synagogues and persecute from town to town, that upon you may come all the righteous blood shed on earth, from the blood of innocent Abel to the blood of Zechariah the son of Barachiah, whom you murdered between the sanctuary and the altar. Truly, I say to you, all this will come upon this generation. (Mt 23:34-36)

Significant here is the universal dimension of the attack. Abel was for the Jewish people the ancestor not simply of the Jews but of all humans, while Zechariah was the last murdered prophet of the bible as Jesus knew it. So Jesus is attacking not just his immediate listeners but religious leaders of all cultures, and not just for the murders of Abel and Zechariah, but for all similar murders since the beginning. The statement 'I send you prophets' implies also that Jesus is revealing this phenomenon on behalf of an observing presence which precedes his earthly life.

The gospel of John is equally explicit in its denunciations:

> 'Why do you not understand what I say? It is because you cannot bear to hear my word. You are of your father the devil, and your will is to do your father's desires. He was a murderer from the beginning, and has nothing to do with the truth, because there is no truth in him. When he lies, he speaks according to his own nature, for he is a liar and the father of lies.' (Jn 8:43-44)

'He was a murderer from the beginning' is clearly a reference to Cain's murder of Abel. The lie is the concealment of the truth about the ritual murder that has just taken place—Cain had asked 'Am I my brother's keeper?' The purpose of ancient religion was the concealment of the truth that it had been founded upon murder, so those whom religion empowers are party to this lie. And to conceal it they are prepared to murder those who point it out. But Jesus is unremitting:

> Woe to you lawyers! for you have taken away the key
> of knowledge; you did not enter yourselves and you
> hindered those who were entering. (Lk 11:52)

It follows that Jesus is revealing 'things hidden since the beginning of the world' (Mt 13:35)—specifically the foundation of human culture upon the concealment of murder. This is the key of knowledge, revealing the role of violence in founding religion and culture. But Jesus is to reveal this not simply by stating it verbally. He himself will fall victim to the same process, through the anger his words cause:

> As he went away from there, the scribes and the Pharisees
> began to press him hard, and to provoke him to speak of
> many things, lying in wait for him, to catch at something
> he might say. (Lk 11:53)

They are determined again to take away the key of knowledge, but can think of only one means to do so, the old means used throughout history—to repeat the original murder. The crucifixion of this particular victim, clearly free of mimetic desire and of all personal ambition, will reveal the injustice of all scapegoating.

The proof of the success of this revelation comes in the story of Stephen, who recapitulates precisely the same process by simply pointing out what has happened.

'You stiff-necked people, uncircumcised in heart and ears, you always resist the Holy Spirit. As your fathers did, so do you. Which of the prophets did not your fathers persecute? And they killed those who announced beforehand the coming of the Righteous One, who you have now betrayed and murdered, you who received the law as delivered by angels and did not keep it.' Now when they heard these things they were enraged, and they ground their teeth against him. But he, full of the Holy Spirit, gazed into heaven and saw the glory of God, and Jesus standing at the right hand of God; and he said, 'Behold, I see the heavens opened, and the Son of man standing at the right hand of God.' But they cried out with a loud voice and stopped their ears and rushed together upon him. Then they cast him out of the city and stoned him. (Acts 7:51-58)

Here again the reaction to Stephen's accusation is to repeat the very process of which he reminds his murderers. The turning of the key of knowledge triggers a reaction designed to bury it, which confirms its revelatory power. However, Stephen's death also reveals that Christ's death will not in itself prevent further recurrences, because we humans will always be free to repeat the same scapegoating processes. Freedom to repent implies also freedom to conceal the key of knowledge, to bury it again by further murders.

Girard's conviction that all ancient cultures were founded on scapegoating violence is accepted by many experts in his field who would not share his belief that the bible is categorically different from all other ancient texts. Yet, once pointed out, the specifically biblical revelation of, and intolerance for, scapegoating violence is striking. Here we have another compelling explanation, standing apart from conventional Christian theology, of the downward journey and crucifixion of Jesus: it was a revelation of the origin of all ancient cultures in concealed murder, and therefore an attempt to found culture on something else—the spirit in which he died—of total love and forgiveness, and recognition of those who suffer. On the cross forever they are, with him, exalted. This divine recognition of the pain of humanity is the only cultural resource humankind possesses that can carry us through the utter injustice of the world of the upward journey. Without that unique downward journey we are condemned to scapegoating violence forever.

CHAPTER VI

Origins of the Western Chasm

How did Christ's revelation of the key of knowledge—man's tendency to found religion and culture upon murder—so clearly recorded by the bible, become obscured in western culture, even within the Christian tradition? That it did so is clear both from the historical record of the middle ages, in which the church became complicit, even instrumental, in the murder of heretics and infidels, and in the modern period, when a highly educated nation could—in the name of German nationalism—rationally plan and undertake the genocide of the very nation through whom the key had been revealed.

To answer this question we need to summarise some history. From the first to the early fourth century, Christianity spread throughout the Mediterranean world, unified as never before by the Roman Empire whose greatest virtue was its tolerance, albeit imperfect, of religious plurality. Christianity was not entirely uniform in its beliefs, structures and practices, but grew by virtue of its appeal to those alienated from the confusion of paganism, and drawn to a life of self-discipline, charity and piety. The contradictory essence of the faith, and its ability to free the person from the vanities of the upward journey, survived, as is illustrated in the following description of Christians from the *Epistle to Diognetus* of the second or third century:

They marry, as do all; they beget children; but they do not destroy their offspring. They have a common table, but not a common bed. They are in the flesh, but they do not live after the flesh. They pass their days on earth, but they are citizens of heaven. They obey the prescribed laws, and at the same time surpass the laws by their lives. They love all men, and are persecuted by all. They are unknown and condemned; they are put to death, and restored to life. They are poor, yet make many rich; they are in lack of all things, and yet abound in all; they are dishonoured, and yet in their very dishonour are glorified. They are evil spoken of, and yet are justified; they are reviled, and bless; they are insulted, and repay the insult with honour; they do good, yet are punished as evildoers. When punished, they rejoice as if quickened into life; they are assailed by the Jews as foreigners, and are persecuted by the Greeks; yet those who hate them are unable to assign any reason for their hatred.[2]

It is clear from this that the contradictory ethic of the original followers of Christ had survived his death by at least two centuries. 'They love all men, and are persecuted by all' — this could stand as a summary of an ideal for all time. And the very orderliness of the lives of Christians made them successful in worldly terms also. By the early fourth century:

Christianity had become in many striking ways a mirror-image of the empire itself. It was catholic, universal, ecumenical, orderly, international, multi-racial and increasingly legalistic. It was administered by a professional class of literates who in some ways functioned like bureaucrats, and its bishops, like imperial governors, legates or prefects, had wide discretionary powers to interpret the law. It was becoming the Doppelganger of the empire. In attacking and weakening it, the empire was debilitating itself.[3]

The obvious solution was for the empire first to legalise Christianity, then to give it the status of state church. But what would happen to Christianity itself if Christians lost their status as a persecuted minority, and became not merely tolerated but privileged? This question was answered in the aftermath of the Edict of Milan of 313 CE, in which the Emperor Constantine declared the freedom of Christians to practise their faith throughout the empire. When he granted to the Christian clergy the same status, emolument and fiscal privilege as had attached to the pagan priests, clerical status soared and became itself a source of bitter conflict. Ammianus records that in 366 CE a disputed election for bishop of Rome left 137 dead in one church. He explained that the bishops of Rome:

> are free from money worries, enriched by offerings from married women, riding in carriages, dressing splendidly, feasting luxuriantly—their banquets are better than imperial ones.[4]

It is clear from this that, as soon as it gained state patronage, Christianity itself had immediately embarked, especially among its clergy, upon the upward journey. This journey would take it to wealth and power which, by the eleventh century, would make the popes, in the view of their most sycophantic theologians, a supreme authority, uniting all temporal and spiritual power.

Worse, far worse was the fact that this upward journey would, like all such journeys, involve new victims. The initial victims were the pagans. St Ambrose explained to the Emperor Valentinian I why the pagan high priest deserved no hearing:

> But, says he, let the altars be restored to the images, and their ornaments to the shrines. Let this demand be made

of one who shares in their superstitions; a Christian Emperor has learnt to honour the altar of Christ alone. Why do they exact of pious hands and faithful lips the ministry to their sacrilege? Let the voice of our Emperor utter the Name of Christ alone, and speak of Him only, Whom he is conscious of, for the King's heart is in the hand of the Lord. Has any heathen Emperor raised an altar to Christ? While they demand the restoration of things which have been, by their own example they show us how great reverence Christian Emperors ought to pay to the religion which they follow, since heathen ones offered all to their superstitions.[5]

The implication is clear. The separation of church and state, implicit and explicit in the teachings and death of Jesus, is to be abandoned immediately upon the church's promotion to the status of state church. The Empire is to be Christian, which means that Christianity will accept the new pyramid of esteem which places Christianity in a dominant position. Pagans will suffer the proscription once enjoyed by the Christians, losing their temples and their freedom to worship. Christianity of the upward journey is to be almost as partisan as paganism had ever been, setting no new standard of tolerance. So, inevitably, Christian victims will be replaced by pagan ones, at the hand of a Christian Emperor. This is the beginning of the process whereby Christianity, in becoming powerful in the human sense, alienated itself from its own roots and inspiration. The alienation would never be complete, but this was not for want of trying.

What Ambrose did for the pagans, Augustine of Hippo would do for Christian dissidents. At first convinced that belief must be a free act, he pledged to a Donatist bishop in 388 CE:

'On our part let the terror cease which is caused by the civil powers . . . let us use reason to settle our differences . . .'[6]

Yet he later abandoned this position and supported suppression:

> 'Because I had not yet seen either how much evil their (i.e. the Donatists') lack of restraint would cause, or how effective solid discipline would be in changing them for the better.'[7]

Here we see in the mind that dominated the middle ages an administrator's preference for 'solid discipline', which included confiscations, imprisonment and other forms of coercion, over freedom of belief, which Augustine, as a theologian, contrarily also verbally upheld. How innocuous the transition sounds, until we reflect that the Inquisition would grow naturally out of Augustine's rethink on religious freedom, and the clerical presumption of a greater wisdom to be imposed for the greater good. The enormous reputation that Augustine won for his defence of the Christian establishment in *The City of God* is based, at best, upon clerical paternalism — the conviction that the clergy, patronised by the state, should determine religious policy and discourse.

It is argued on Augustine's behalf that the doctrine of conscience evolved only slowly to Aquinas' position that even an erroneous conscience was morally compelling, and that Augustine by contrast believed the opposite. Yet the fact remained that the church, which embraced the union of church and state for the next millennium and a half, became deeply ambivalent about human freedom.

The roots of this betrayal of the crucified Christ lie in the new vistas that lay before the hierarchy of the newly promoted church. For Augustine, the church was a house abuilding which would soon dominate the earth.

> Tell it out among the nations, that the Lord reigneth from the wood (i.e. the cross): and that it is He who hath made the round world so fast that it cannot be moved. What testimonies of the building of the house of God! The clouds of heaven thunder out throughout the world

that God's house is being built; and the frogs cry from the
marsh, 'We alone are Christians'.[8]

Two things are noteworthy here: Augustine's vision of the final dominance
of the church, and, by contrast, his contempt for the Donatists as frogs
crying from the marsh. The 'house' of Augustine became Christendom.
Augustine is pivotal in the church's transformation from minority
fellowship before Constantine into a power structure determined to retain
and expand its temporal power.

And so, of course, Augustine could watch unmoved as under
oppression these Christian dissidents, these frogs who stood in the way of
his and the church's upward journey, would commit mass suicide rather
than yield. Their opposition to orthodoxy had placed them at the base
of Augustine's pyramid of esteem, and they paid, under the gaze of this
great churchman, the price that Christ had paid, apparently fruitlessly.

The means by which he argued himself into this position were
important also. Writing to a Donatist who had argued that 'no man should
be compelled to that which is good', Augustine insisted:

> When you threw yourself the other day into a well, in
> order to bring death upon yourself, you did so no doubt
> with your free will. But how cruel the servants of God
> would have been if they had left you to the fruits of this
> bad will, and had not delivered you from that death! Who
> would not have justly blamed them? Who would not
> have justly denounced them as inhuman? And yet you,
> with your own free will, threw yourself into the water
> that you might be drowned. They took you against your
> will out of the water, that you might not be drowned. You
> acted according to your own will, but with a view to your
> destruction; they dealt with you against your will, but
> in order to your preservation. If, therefore, mere bodily
> safety behoves to be so guarded that it is the duty of those

who love their neighbour to preserve him even against his own will from harm, how much more is this duty binding in regard to that spiritual health in the loss of which the consequence to be dreaded is eternal death![9]

St Paul's conversion is interpreted to the same purpose:

If a bad will ought always to be left to its own freedom, why was Paul not left to the free use of that most perverted will with which he persecuted the church? Why was he thrown to the ground that he might be blinded, and struck blind that he might be changed, and changed that he might be sent as an apostle, and sent that he might suffer for the truth's sake such wrongs as he had inflicted on others when he was in error?[10]

And here is how Augustine argued his church into systematic oppression:

I hear that you have remarked and often quote the fact recorded in the gospels, that the seventy disciples went back from the Lord, and that they had been left to their own choice in this wicked and impious desertion, and that to the twelve who alone remained the Lord said, 'Will ye also go away?' But you have neglected to remark, that at that time the church was only beginning to burst into life from the recently planted seed, and that there was not yet fulfilled in her the prophecy: *'All kings shall fall down before Him; yea, all nations shall serve Him'*; and it is in proportion to the more enlarged accomplishment of this prophecy that the church wields greater power, so that she may not only invite, but even compel men to embrace what is good. This our Lord intended then to illustrate, for although He had great power, He chose rather to manifest His humility. This also He taught, with sufficient plainness, in the parable of the Feast, in which the master of the house, after He had sent a message to the invited guests, and they had refused to come, said to his servants: *'Go out quickly into the streets and lanes of the city, and bring in hither the poor, and the maimed, and the halt, and the blind.'* And the servant said, 'Lord, it is done as thou hast commanded, and yet there is room.' And the Lord said unto the servant, *'Go out into the highways and hedges, and compel them to come in, that my house may be filled.'* Mark, now, how it was said in regard to those who came first, 'bring them in'; it was not said, 'compel them to come in,' by which was signified the incipient condition of the church, when it was only growing towards the position in which it would have strength to compel men to come in. Accordingly, because it was right that when the church had been strengthened, both in power and in extent, men should be compelled to come in to the feast of everlasting salvation, it was afterwards added in the parable, 'The servant said, "Lord, it is done as thou hast commanded, and yet there is room." And the Lord said unto the servants, *"Go out into the highways and hedges, and compel them to come in."* Wherefore, if you were walking peaceably, absent from this feast of everlasting salvation and of the holy unity of the church, we should find you, as it were, in the 'highways'; but since, by multiplied injuries and cruelties, which you perpetrate on our people, you are, as it were, full of thorns and roughness, we find you as it were in the 'hedges', and we compel you to come in. The sheep which is compelled is driven whither it would not wish to go, but after it has entered, it feeds of its own accord in the pastures to which it was brought. Wherefore restrain your perverse and rebellious spirit, that in the true church of Christ you may find the feast of salvation.[11]

It would be a mistake to attribute gross insensitivity to this lecturing of a man clearly at the end of his tether (his name, coincidentally, was Donatus). Augustine is in fact lecturing the church universal, using this instance of opposition to declare what he hoped would become its established policy. An exegesis based upon the dignity and forbearance of 'Will you too go away?' is rejected, quite arbitrarily, in favour of a plainly self-indulgent exegesis based upon 'Compel them to come in!', as though 'compel' necessarily meant 'coerce', rather than 'persuade'. Upon this quite arbitrary choice turned the lives of countless thousands of humans in the centuries that followed. 'Compel them to come in!' became the very foundation of religious murder for over fifteen centuries.

It is worth noticing here also how Augustine argued that 'Will you too go away?' could only be the church's policy in a time of relative weakness. A powerful church—one to which kings would bow the knee—had no need of such a policy. Augustine's brilliant mind had clearly been confused by the church's upward journey, and by his heady visions of what it would yet become. Here we find the root of the alienation of the modern mind from its Christian origins.

Thus the record shows that, at the first opportunity to demonstrate from a position of power its solidarity with all victims, the church leadership failed, and went on doing so. The church's political upward journey peaked in 1076 CE when pope Gregory VII compelled Henry IV, whom he had excommunicated and deposed for investing bishops, to stand for three days in the snow at Canossa. However, the full horror of what could follow from a papacy wedded to political power was revealed at the end of the same century, when, according to one account, Pope Urban II asked at Clermont in 1095:

> Can anyone tolerate that we (Europeans) do not even
> share equally with the Moslems the inhabited earth?
> They have made Asia, which is a third of the world, their
> homeland . . . They have also forcibly held Africa, the
> second portion of the world, for over 200 years. There
> remains Europe, the third continent. How small a portion
> of it is inhabited by us Christians.[12]

The solution to this, and to Europe's own internal violence and land hunger, was the First Crusade, culminating in the taking of Jerusalem in 1099. Four centuries earlier, when the Caliph Umar had taken Jerusalem from the Christians, he had refused to pray in the church of the Holy Sepulchre lest he give offence to Christians and tempt his own followers to seize it. He had then signed a peace agreement which gave the Christians: 'security for their lives, property, churches, and the crucifixes belonging to those who display and honour them . . . There shall be no compulsion in matters of faith.'[13]

Now in the same Jerusalem in 1099, according to the Christian Fulcheron of Chartres: 'Our Squires and footmen . . . split open the bellies of those they had just slain in order to extract from the intestines the gold coins which the Saracens had gulped down their loathsome throats while alive . . . With drawn swords our men ran through the city not sparing anyone, even those begging for mercy.'[14]

Virtually all in the city, women and children not excepted, perished. The Jewish population was exterminated by setting fire to the synagogue in which all had taken refuge. Those few Saracens who survived were employed in a manner foreshadowing the years 1942-45:

> They also ordered that all the corpses of the Saracens
> should be thrown outside the city because of the fearful
> stench; for almost the whole city was full of their dead
> bodies. The Saracens who were still alive dragged the
> dead ones out in front of the gates, and made piles of

them, as big as houses. Such a slaughter of pagans no one
has ever seen or heard of; the pyres they made were like
pyramids.[15]

An estimated 40,000 Muslims and Jews died in a manner that can be explained
only in terms of a complete suspension of reason and compassion—the
hallmarks of the scapegoating violence which the bible and the crucifixion
had so clearly exposed. And this was done at the behest of a Catholic pope
and Christian clergy.

The church was not immediately abashed however. The apex of its
intellectual inflation came with the *Polycraticus* of John of Salisbury almost
a century later:

> The prince therefore, as very many assert, is the public
> authority, and a certain image of the divine majesty on
> earth . . . Therefore, the prince receives this sword from
> the head of the church, since she herself would never
> wield the sword of force. However she has it and she uses
> it through the hand of the ruler on whom she confers the
> power of keeping persons within limits, though keeping
> for herself the authority of spiritual things in her Pontiffs.
> Wherefore it is that the chief authority seems unsuited for
> the hand of a priest . . . Certainly, as is witnessed by the
> testimony of the Teacher of the Gentiles, he who blesses
> is greater than he who is blessed; and the authority with
> which the dignity has been conferred distinguishes the
> spiritual power insofar as it has been placed under it by
> God, namely, in those things which pertain to the salvation
> of the soul, and therefore in these things the spiritual
> power must be obeyed rather than the secular power.
> In those things which pertain to the civil welfare the
> secular authority must be obeyed rather than the spiritual
> authority, in accordance with Matthew 22: 'Render to

> Caesar the things that are Caesar's, etc.,' unless perhaps
> the secular power is joined to the spiritual power, as in
> the pope, who holds the summit of each power, namely
> spiritual and secular.[16]

This was the final intellectual fulfilment of the grand Augustinian vision, that climb to moral dominance that had begun in the matrix of the pagan Roman Empire. It was to produce yet further victims, however. In 1209, in pursuit of the Albigensians, 'Arnold Aimery exulted to the pope that the capture of Beziers had been "miraculous"; and that these crusaders had killed 15,000 "showing mercy neither to order, nor age nor sex".'[17]

We do not need to labour the point by recounting all the horrors of the Middle Ages (although it is spiritually necessary for all Christians to revisit these events, as well as the passion of Christ). In defence of the church it can be said that heresy itself perpetrated atrocities, and that the church was reliant upon a secular power that often lacked discipline and order. However, the fact remains that in the era of the church's greatest political and social influence, bloody and systematic murder was often done in the name of Christ, and that this was in the end a decisive factor in the alienation of western civilisation from the same Christ. In embarking, under Augustine's influence, upon the upward journey to power, the church had effectively buried the truth that in the Christ of the downward journey lay the only solution to the problem of religious violence.

There is a key truth in all of this that needs to be emphasised. When someone is killed in the name of truth, the truth that is upheld is one which denies the right of that individual to intellectual and religious freedom. This is not Christian truth, but Christian falsehood, since Christ deliberately rejected the option of the use of force. In setting out to exterminate heresy of doctrine, Augustine, and all clerics of the same overbearing journey, were perpetrating a heresy of praxis which would teach the world to associate Christ with violence—the ultimate betrayal of his real purpose. No heresy of the word was ever greater than this.

CHAPTER VII

Downward Journeys

The reasons typically given by historians for the decline of the western church, from about 1200 CE, do not concern us here. What matters is that this descent was, in the end, salutary and providential, from a Christian perspective, as it stripped from the papacy the worldly power it had acquired in contradiction of Jesus' downward journey.

Already weakened by the forced removal of the popes to Avignon in 1309, and the Black Death of the mid-fourteenth century, the papacy lost further prestige in the Great Western Schism of 1378-1417. The crusades had not only degraded Christianity generally, but greatly strengthened the separation of the eastern and western churches. And the hubris of the western church suffered another devastating blow in 1517, when Martin Luther began his protest against indulgences and other perceived corruptions in the western church. There followed almost two centuries of conflict inspired by religious hatred.

Coincidentally there was a reawakening of the European mind from about 1450. This was inspired by a renewed interest in the classical civilisations of Greece and Rome, and by western voyages of global exploration. The rediscovery of the truth that Athens and Rome had created orderly societies without the church, and the discovery of foreign lands that the bible knew nothing of, raised questions about the intellectual authority of the church. The printing press removed the reproduction of information from the control of clergy, and enabled a far more rapid spread of information and ideas to a far wider readership. Religious wars, and the memory of religious violence over centuries, equally questioned the churches' moral authority. The silencing of Galileo, however it may now be defended, was another devastating blow to both, setting the scene for a western ideological assault upon Christianity per se. Even before Newton the alienation of the western mind from Christianity, and the rise of what we call secularism, were well under way.

The 'Enlightenment'

Isaac Newton's *Principia*, published in 1687, had probably more impact on the modern world than any other work, including the bible. Newton had discovered some of the most important laws of physics, including those that took man to the moon in 1969. The western mind woke up to the power of natural scientific laws. *'To every action there is an equal and opposite reaction.'* This, Newton's third law of motion, explains why an inflated balloon, released without tying the neck, will fly off in the direction opposite to the escape of air through the neck itself. It is also the principle behind the rockets that launched the Apollo missions into space less than two centuries after Newton's revolution.

Using these basic laws of motion and gravitation, Newton was able to solve a problem that had baffled scientists of his time: why Earth, and the other planets that make up our solar system, orbit the sun—a perpetual journey around the source of warmth and light and life itself. He explained this in terms of a balance between two forces: the gravitational attraction of the sun upon the earth, and the earth's own velocity or speed through space, which tends to take it away from the sun. Moreover he was able to prove his theory mathematically, and insisted that the laws he had discovered were natural laws that applied throughout the universe, as well as upon Earth itself.

This scientific revelation astonished the most intelligent men of Newton's time and, in the aftermath of the Galileo affair, further undermined the authority of the Catholic Church. If profound truths unknown to the church could be discovered by unaided human observation, experiment, insight, logic and mathematics—the tools of reason—what value had religious faith? The most dramatic Christian claims about the existence of a personal God who had intervened in the history of mankind could not be proven by the same 'scientific' method, so what status had they?

Probably the most influential reader of Newton was the French writer, Voltaire—not a scientist but a propagandist for the application of 'reason' in all spheres of knowledge and life. He became chief spokesman for the 'Enlightenment', an intellectual movement which dominated the eighteenth century and shaped the whole idea of modernity. Its purpose was to make 'reason', not religious faith, the basis of European culture. Its leaders, the *'philosophes '*, were convinced that the natural laws of physics discovered by Newton were merely the first to be discovered of many other similar laws governing other branches of knowledge, and simply waiting to be identified. They believed they were on the brink of a universal understanding, that reason was the only key to knowledge and would soon unlock all of it.

Among those other areas of knowledge were the nature of man and society, until then largely monopolised by the churches. The 'Enlightenment' became convinced that, applied to these, reason would reveal similar scientific laws which would make theology and the churches redundant. Profoundly optimistic about man released from clerical obscurantism, the 'Enlightenment' challenged the whole concept of sin, particularly original sin. The only basic evils, they argued, were ignorance and confusion, which they charged the clergy with deliberately exploiting in order to maintain their own monopoly of thought. Out of this belief arose branches of science unknown until then—including economics, psychology, political science, sociology and anthropology. Out of these in turn emerged the ideologies which caused such havoc in the twentieth century.

An essential component in the 'Enlightenment's reaction against institutional Christianity was a reaction against the history of religious violence which had followed the union of church and state in Europe in the fourth century. Voltaire, in his *Dictionary of Philosophy*, portrayed Christ as wringing his hands over the mounds of human bones resulting from the persecution of heresy, the crusades, the burning of witches, the work of the Inquisition (still operating in Spain in the era of the 'Enlightenment') and the wars of religion which had followed the Protestant Reformation and Counter (i.e. Catholic) Reformation in the 1500s. 'Crush the infamy!' was his attitude towards institutional Christianity, in particular the Catholic Church. Clerics were from that point on generally on the defensive, no longer capable of forming the minds of most intellectuals of the West.

Applied to technology, science and reason had spectacular success. The best early example was the Watt steam engine, first applied not to the problem of transport but to powering other machines, such as the spinning and weaving machines of the cotton industry in England. These and other similar developments began the industrial revolutions of the nineteenth and twentieth centuries, which brought about the fastest social changes in the whole of human history. The steam engine did for the nineteenth century what the microchip will do for the twenty-first—and both are owed to the scientific attitude towards knowledge that began with the 'Enlightenment'. The idea of progress, expected in all areas of life, began to dominate not only the intelligentsia, but popular culture also.

In the aftermath of the French Revolution, the Catholic Church scored another spectacular own-goal by siding with the forces of political reaction against the principle of democracy. The future lay as much with democracy in the world of politics as it did with science in the realm of education. In alienating both, the church was guaranteeing the advance of secularism. Slow to detach itself from the principle of slavery, it also suffered by rejecting the principle of religious freedom. Until Napoleon's armies marched into the Papal States in the early years of the nineteenth century, Jewish ghettos had existed there. As a result, few sympathised with the papacy when it lost most of its territorial independence to the advance of Italian nationalism by 1870.

Meanwhile the power of technology to change and control our material circumstances necessarily also undermined the sense of being at the mercy of uncontrollable forces such as weather patterns, which had periodically caused famines throughout Europe. Advances in medical science showed that human disease might also be scientifically controllable. Reliance upon God to 'deliver us from evil' tended to be replaced by faith in science. The status of the cleric necessarily plummeted as that of the scientist rose.

Another hammer blow struck the churches in 1859, as a direct consequence of the 'Enlightenment', when the biologist Charles Darwin advanced the theory that all species of life were subject to very gradual change through vast periods of time, as the result of the success of slight genetic variations in helping particular strains to survive. He pointed out the similarity between the physiology of man and that of primates, implying an evolutionary relationship and the gradual emergence of all forms of life from more primitive forms. The implications of this appeared to contradict the biblical account of creation. Another new science, geology, pointed to other evidence that Earth was not just about 4,000 years old, as the bible seemed to suggest, but many millions, and that the many different layers of rock and clay beneath man's feet testified to the truth of slow evolutionary change over this vast period.

Meanwhile the industrial revolutions of the west had led to an age of European imperialism, a secular upward journey which made Europe, by the mid-nineteenth century, master of the world in economic and military terms. However, the rise of the USA, and the great wars of the twentieth century, brought an end to this era, and encouraged the spread of anti-European nationalisms to what had been European colonies.

In the twentieth century, the 'Enlightenment' delivered another series of shocks to Christendom. Freud, the greatest single influence on the science of psychology, insisted upon the baneful influence of Christian sexual repression upon the health of the human psyche. In so doing he began a revolution in western attitudes to sexuality which eventually deprived celibate Catholic clergy of their last ideological lever. Freud also dismissed religion as a neurotic fantasy based upon infantile longing for an authoritarian parent. This seemed even more persuasive when cultural anthropologists later pointed to the strong similarity of some of the bible texts to other ancient foundation myths, suggesting that all were simply manifestations of the human psyche and ancient culture, with no revelatory power and no profound message for twentieth-century humanity.

These developments all combined to persuade many in the educated classes in the West of the unlikelihood of the existence of a non-material being with human sympathies who had intervened in human history, most notably through divine incarnation in the man Jesus. Many others, although unable to contest the findings of science, argued that religion had an important moral and cultural role, and so could not be simply jettisoned. So, both the rational outlook and the churches survived, but the latter were badly shaken and generally in retreat. Only fundamentalism—a rejection of the scientific outlook in favour of a literalist interpretation of the bible—thrived, at the expense of an even wider chasm between the western mind and the downward journey of Jesus. The Christian view of the world was gradually displaced by a secular cast of mind in almost all aspects of life. The average Christian in the west came to live mentally in two different worlds—the Sunday world of God, sin and redemption, and the weekday world which knew nothing of these and was increasingly governed by the attitudes of the 'Enlightenment' and the values of the expanding global market.

The latter world is the world of the secular, that is, of all that is non-religious. The normal discourse of this world has to do with the problem of making a living in an increasingly technological culture. It tends to be embarrassed by, and even hostile to, talk of the spiritual, the non-material—matters not subject to observation, measurement and control.

Thus, religious claims to important truth are under attack on two fronts: for being a potential source of violence, and for being intellectually unverifiable and obscurantist.

However, as we have seen, the political and economic ideologies which emerged from the 'Enlightenment', together with all of the human and political sciences, did not fulfil the expectations of the *philosophes*. The century of technological marvels just ended was also the century of greatest human violence and suffering, by an enormous margin, largely due to improvements in the technology of death. The 'Enlightenment' had entrusted the fate of man to science, but scientists too were corruptible by the upward journey of nations—turning their attention to the invention of weapons such as breech-loading rifles and artillery, machine guns and poison gas. In the trenches of World War I, these slaughtered young men in their millions. Tanks and military aircraft appeared for the first time, and proved their potential for mass slaughter in World War 2.

The ideologies that justified these wars also originated in the 'Enlightenment'. Nationalism assured young men all over Europe in 1914 that they would be in one another's capital cities by Christmas. It was also the fundamental driving force of German expansion that caused World War 2. It still plagues the Balkans and the Middle East. And socialism justified a programme of mass terror in eastern Europe from 1917 until 1953.

And the ultimate cost of our extraordinary technical advance in the west is an endangered environment for which the greatest economic powers as yet take no global responsibility. Extolling the benefits of individual ownership of an eternally expanding array of consumer goods, we have adopted and globalised a lifestyle of material profligacy on a scale which, as a model for the developing world, promises certain global disaster.

Thus, the extraordinary enthusiasm generated by the early 'Enlightenment' has evaporated. The confidence that reason could build Utopia has been replaced by a drug-induced flight from reality among our young.

Moreover, the progress of reason itself has undermined the optimism of the 'Enlightenment' by questioning the possibility of us humans ever arriving at what used to be called absolute truth. Since the existence of a God cannot be proved by reason, the existence of absolute objective truth is equally questionable. All truth must be said to be relative, dependent upon the mentality and culture and experience and era of the individual. This pessimism about the whole human project, and about our ability to know anything for sure about anything, is broadly termed 'post-modernism'. The sheer nihilism of the term is itself evidence of reason at the end of its tether.

At the end of the second millennium we therefore find both faith and reason, both Christendom and secularism, bereft of confidence about the future. Both are situated spiritually at the terminus of historical arcs which led them upwards, willingly, towards intellectual and political dominance and hubris, then, unwillingly, downwards towards an unprecedented and simultaneous crisis of faith. Confident Christianity has become almost the monopoly, and thus the victim, of fundamentalism, which serves simply to deepen the chasm between secularism and Christianity. The west's economic ascendancy continues, but we have almost lost direction and idealism.

We are therefore spiritually ready to understand the full implications of Jesus' downward journey, which bridges all chasms.

CHAPTER VIII

Bridging the Chasm between Faith and Freedom

At Christmas 1998, the Irish journalist David Quinn wrote a piece for the *Sunday Times* entitled 'Keep the Faith—but you also have to keep the dogma'. He recounted a conversation with an Irish TV executive who had asked him how the Catholic church leadership was to recover any influence in Ireland following a series of scandals. Quinn had responded by suggesting that the church would need to more clearly explain its core teachings or dogma. This suggestion was summarily dismissed. 'People today have no time for dogma,' his interlocutor told him. 'Dogma is what's ruining religion.' Quinn went on:

> 'My interrogator . . . expressed a typically modern impatience with the whole concept of dogma. Dogma fuelled the Inquisition. It burnt women at the stake for witchcraft. It caused bloody and long-running religious wars across Europe. Dogmatic religion was responsible for the St Bartholomew's Day massacre in France in 1572 when Catholics killed Protestants in their thousands.'

Quinn's article did not deny these charges, but went on to argue that reason, for him the alternative to dogma, had not brought intellectual agreement and couldn't inspire lives of service. 'Do away with dogma, with defining beliefs, and you do away with the ideals that motivate people to go out and change the world.' He went on:

> 'Agnosticism never energised anyone. It never sparked a mass movement or started a religion. History has shown that once a movement starts to doubt itself, it starts to die. That is why liberal Christianity is failing so badly. It has decided that only religion without dogma has a future.'

Is this then the choice that faces Ireland and the West? To revert to dogmatism, accepting its downside—intolerance and authoritarianism, maybe even a murderous fanaticism—or to adopt a vague self-indulgent liberalism without clear core beliefs? If so we haven't moved from the situation described by Yeats in *The Second Coming*, written early this century.

> Things fall apart, the centre cannot hold;
> Mere anarchy is loosed upon the world.
> The blood-dimmed tide is loosed, and everywhere
> The ceremony of innocence is drowned;
> The best lack all conviction, while the worst
> are full of passionate intensity.[18]

This exchange between Quinn and his RTE acquaintance goes to the heart of the dilemma of the west. The nub of the problem is clear. It is the belief, held both by liberals and by conservative Christians, that dogma cannot embrace freedom, and that freedom cannot embrace a passionate Christian faith. If this perception is accurate, then Christian dogma cannot contain the principle of religious freedom as a core belief, and those who believe passionately in freedom cannot believe strongly in anything else, for fear of becoming dogmatic.

Dogma cannot embrace freedom?

Let us begin by taking the first part of this position—that a passionate Christianity cannot embrace the principle of human freedom. It is true that from the late fourth to the late nineteenth century the Catholic Church denied, often murderously, the principle of religious freedom. As late as 1864 Pope Pius IX's Syllabus (or List) of Errors indicted the 'mad' principle of religious liberty and went on:

> Therefore do we, by our apostolic authority, reprobate, denounce and condemn generally and particularly all the evil opinions and doctrines specially mentioned in this letter, and we wish and command that they be held as reprobated, denounced and condemned by all the children of the Catholic Church.[19]

This couldn't be clearer. Yet by 1965 the same church, embodied in Vatican Council II, had declared in a document devoted specifically to this issue, *The Declaration on Religious Freedom*:

> The truth cannot impose itself except by virtue of its own truth, as it makes its entrance into the mind with both gentleness and power.[20]

This newly discovered principle—a categorical repudiation of Augustine's justification of religious coercion—became the basis of the church's current appeals for religious freedom throughout the world, particularly where Catholics are in a minority position, ranging from eastern Europe to India, Pakistan and China.

Where did this principle come from? Certainly not from the church's practice or policy over one and a half millennia. And not from the text of the gospels either, it seems, for no scriptural citation was given at this point in the Vatican II document, although everything else that can be sourced there is meticulously annotated in all of the council documents. We have here a mystery of derivation. Liberalism, originating in the Enlightenment, took it as axiomatic that religious freedom was a basic human right as early as the mid-1700s. The Catholic Church did not assent to this for another two centuries. The connection appears to be Fr John Courtney Murray SJ, who drafted the Vatican II document. He had earlier argued that the basic rights enshrined in the US constitution, including freedom of belief, were compatible with Christianity (*We Hold these Truths*).[21] And, as everyone knows, the US constitution is an eighteenth century document heavily influenced by the 'Enlightenment'. To be fair to Murray, the main argument upon which he based the principle of religious freedom related to the natural law, a concept very old in the church. God, he argued, had given freedom to all to reach their supernatural goal, so this justified the granting of freedom of conscience to all believers by the state, irrespective of their denomination. The Vatican II declaration also stated that religious intolerance was contrary to the 'spirit of the gospels'.

There is an important problem here. The church now accepts as axiomatic the principle of religious freedom — but seems to have derived it from the 'Enlightenment' and/or a very late natural law argument, rather than from scripture or tradition as it had been practised and taught for by far the greater part of the church's long history.

The nub of the question is this: does God believe in the principle of religious freedom? According to Murray and the Vatican II church the answer is 'yes', but no clear scriptural basis for this belief has been identified. Why was the church denied a clear revealed truth on this matter for so long, given its divine support? The problem becomes even more pressing when we remember those many thousands of victims of religious intolerance over those centuries. Did God not care about this? If we are to believe John Paul II, God cares profoundly for all of the church's sins of intolerance, but Christ was apparently silent on the issue. This is strange and unsettling, and not overcome by reference to unformed understanding at the time. (The whole point of being a Christian is the belief that one's faith already contains at least most of the truth and can enlighten the understanding of all periods. Was the issue of religious freedom unimportant to Jesus?)

There is another problem that has been gnawing away at Christianity over the centuries. Why was the crucifixion necessary anyway? The doctrine of atonement is supposed to explain this, but no such doctrine has been found completely satisfactory. The classic early notion—that humans were in bondage to the devil and had to be rescued by a human act of great heroism—was countered by the argument, made by St Anselm and others, that God could have ransomed us at a far lower price. Anselm's own notion, still influential, was that God's justice and honour required a reparation for human sin greater than any possible sum total of human virtue, without Jesus' self sacrifice. Yet this was countered by Abelard: wasn't the crucifixion itself the greatest of all human crimes; why did the Father choose to add this to the sum of human infamy, if his intention was to forgive us anyway?

It seems that the crucifixion is still a problem for theologians. Joseph Cardinal Ratzinger, prefect of the Congregation for the Doctrine of the Faith, was the Catholic church's supreme theological monitor during the pontificate of John Paul II. In an extended interview in 1996, discussing the problem of the power of evil, Peter Seewald asked him: 'Does this mean that God has too little power over this world?' The cardinal replied:

> In any case he didn't want to exercise power in the way that we imagine it. This is, of course, exactly the question that I too . . . would ask the 'world-spirit': *Why does he remain so powerless? Why does he reign only in this curiously weak way, as a crucified man, as one who himself failed?* But apparently that is the way he wants to rule; that is the divine form of power. *And the nondivine form of power obviously consists in imposing oneself and getting one's way and coercing.*[22] (My emphasis)

Where a cardinal can with great humility admit a problem, I offer the following solution, both to the problem of deriving religious freedom from the Gospels, and to the problem of understanding the crucifixion:

For both the Father and the Son, the acceptance of crucifixion was necessary because in the end the only alternative was the cancellation of human freedom, the right to reject him, the use by God of what Cardinal Ratzinger calls *the nondivine form of power (which) obviously consists in imposing oneself and getting one's way and coercing.* The Messiah as perceived by the Jews, including Peter, was to be another David, exercising total sovereignty over the lives of all of his subjects, and meeting resistance by force. Christ's acceptance of the sovereignty of Pilate, his rebuke to Peter's use of the sword at Gethsemane, and his consequent acceptance of crucifixion, were in themselves a definitive divine statement of the sovereignty of human freedom, including religious freedom. When we understand to the core of our being that God will suffer rather than coerce us to follow him, then, and only then, are we drawn to Christ by the overwhelming love we must then feel for him. This realisation is also personally devastating, for (no matter how hard we have tried to submit in the past) we have used our freedom until that moment essentially to flee from him, rather than to come close. This personal grief—and it may never be fully overcome in this life—is true repentance, and in that repentance we move freely to the Father, in response to his earlier self-sacrificial movement towards us. The atonement (at-one-ment) then takes place, in the deepest recess of the human heart.

If this explanation is correct, we Catholics who know the history of our church must feel an increased grief in the realisation that all of the church's attempts to draw humankind to Christ, from Augustine on, by the use (or connivance at the use) of force were not only futile, but in practical terms counter-Christian. Here we find the root of the church's present predicament, and not just in Ireland. The church's long alliance with the state, the primary locus of coercive power, was a profound mistake—a vital source of the modern world's alienation from its Christian roots.

How does this relate to the problem of reconciling faith and liberty? A God who believes first and last in human liberty—in Eden and on Calvary—must be loved passionately by anyone who loves freedom, and so must the freedom of all peoples. The clash of dogma with liberty is no more when core dogma includes the principle of liberty. There is no other way of reconciling the two, but, once understood, no other way is needed. The dogma that fuelled the Augustinian upward journey of the church and led to the Crusades and the Inquisition, was warped and incomplete. The defining beliefs that identify the Christian must include faith in the inviolable freedom of the individual human person.

When we trace backward in time the chasm in western culture between freedom and faith, we arrive at Christendom, the notion that state power allied with the truth of Christ can produce a perfect world. It didn't, for the simple reason that the truth of Christ includes the necessary freedom of all men. Without that freedom, atonement—the moment of meeting with God—is impossible for the person who loves freedom (and all men certainly value their own). When the church allies with the state it colludes with *the nondivine form of power (which) obviously consists in imposing oneself and getting one's way and coercing.* The denial of the primacy of human freedom by the church necessarily alienated from it those for whom intellectual and religious freedom were essential. This is the root of the secularist liberal tradition, whose achievements in terms of intellectual and political liberty have shaped our world.

This is why David Quinn and his interlocutor were at odds and could not agree, because Quinn's dogma implicitly minimises the principle of freedom, and must therefore be incomplete. Here we find the root of the problem that Yeats also identified—the separation of passion from faith, and the origin of the 'rough beasts' of the twentieth century, those heartless fanatical ideologies that also tried to build Utopia by force, and produced hell on earth instead. The church's long inability to recognise the principle of freedom left Christians in the Third Reich and in the Soviet Union ambivalent about tyranny.

If we interpret the crucifixion as a rejection of the option of coercion, other passages in the gospel take on an enhanced meaning. When Jesus asked the disciples 'Will you too go away?' we can interpret this—in opposition to Augustine—as an implicit acknowledgement of their freedom and right to do exactly that. Juxtaposed to Thomas Aquinas' implicit approval of torture to compel heretics to recant, it becomes a vindication of the liberal position the church has now adopted. The parables of the lost sheep and the prodigal son can also be interpreted as a divine statement that God's tolerance excels ours.

What alternative position is there? The only obvious one is that God's tolerance is less than ours—an impossible position. When the church in 1965 rejected that option it vindicated, for the first time in 1600 years, the divine tolerance, embarking upon an entirely new relationship with the world. Already committed to the view that the Inquisition was contrary to 'the spirit of the gospels', it needs to see the crucifixion itself as a repudiation of religious coercion, and thus of religious privilege vis-à-vis the state.

It is here, I believe that we find the source of the ambivalence with which many, if not most, well-intentioned people regard the Catholic Church. On the one hand, they see it as a warm enfolding influence, the instrument of God's forgiveness and his grace. On the other, they find it historically tyrannical and overbearing, denying the personal freedom that we find so clearly in the gospel relationships. This ambivalence exists because the church itself, in its historical reality, has been ambivalent, manifesting both the warmth of Jesus and the authoritarianism of Augustine. Neither in the gospels nor in logic is it possible to argue that God is ambivalent: Jesus is non-coercive to the last drop of blood, so coercion has no valid role in Christianity. The central Christian event is a divine acknowledgement of the inalienable freedom of our species.

It makes no sense to argue otherwise. If the crucifixion is to draw all men to the Father, how can the church propose to intrude any other influence into the process of evangelisation? The 'statism' of Catholicism is a fundamental error that has diminished the crucifixion and associated Christ, heretically, with oppression.

Freedom must exclude Dogma?

Finally, let us take the second part of the 'dogma versus freedom' argument: that a passionate belief in human freedom must involve a rejection of dogma. This is simply overcome. A passionate belief in human freedom becomes a liberal dogma when stated as an inalienable belief. If affirmed also by the Christian tradition, we have a mutuality of dogma, of things that are passionately believed, centred upon the principle of human freedom. Had Quinn been able to declare a passionate belief in the religious freedom his church had so long denied, he might have found common ground with his acquaintance. With that fundamental point of conflict resolved, we can then begin to labour together on the great problem of the age—how to reconcile individual freedom with the needs of stable community, without which no-one's liberty is safe.

If history teaches us anything it is that morality and truth cannot be enforced. Nor can faith. The acceptance of dogma can only result from a passionate love of God—and a God who does not love freedom, a God who coerces, is not lovable. The central purpose of this book is to affirm a God for whom human freedom is inviolable.

From this perspective, Christians can rightly claim that modern liberalism is inconceivable outside the context of the Judaeo-Christian tradition, which gave such a high valuation to the individual deprived of dignity by social injustice. As the *Encyclopedia Britannica* recognises, Jesus' Sermon on the Mount affirmed the dignity of, and divine love for, those alienated from the world by poverty and injustice, and must be considered at least one source of modern liberalism. The *Magnificat* and the Christmas story, as well as the personality of the adult Jesus, have deeply influenced western culture, at a level deeper than the intellectual. Even in the Middle Ages peasants typically upbraided their betters by reference to a shared Christian heritage, and affirmed their own dignity by pointing to Jesus' birth in a stable. The 'Enlightenment' did not acknowledge its debt to

Christianity, but this does not mean it had none—specifically compassion for the underdog. The best of the 'Enlightenment' intellectuals expressed a spirit of social concern which goes far beyond mere rationalism. It is not going too far to say that western liberalism also is a branch of the Christian vine, which can also always renew itself by drawing from the same source, for Jesus shows us not only a love for our freedom, but also its most fulfilling use—in service rather than self-indulgence.

We have here a means of interpreting our present crisis which can heal the chasm in western civilisation between secularism and Christianity. Secularism can be seen as the product of an impossible choice forced upon modernity by an obscurantist Christian clergy who misrepresented the Christian God as fundamentally hostile to individual intellectual and personal freedom. In forcing modernity to choose between faith and freedom they effectively secularised the present, misrepresenting Christ himself. However, a Jesus who unaccountably used his freedom to undertake a journey of ultimate self-sacrifice and humiliation, radically challenges the secularist individualism of our culture, the fundamental source of its present danger.

There is absolutely no doubt that unless we can all become wiser as individuals our civilisation is unviable. Lower consumption by the well-to-do, a spirit of service and affirmation of the weak, a tolerant love of all other individuals on the planet, whatever their race or religious persuasion—all these are essential virtues for saving our civilisation. Their outstanding moral archetype, freed from the institutional propaganda of all those organisations which have misrepresented him for their own purposes, is Jesus of Nazareth.

CHAPTER IX

Bridging the Chasm Between Individual and Community

The upward journey threatens community by turning the individual's attention inward towards personal achievement, away from the needs of others. The rampant individualism of the late twentieth century, intensified by the market's insistence that fulfilment lies in the acquisition of more and more 'personal' technology, is challenging communities everywhere. And so it is challenging individuals also, since without a strong sense of community no-one is safe. Individualism, the exclusively upward personal journey, threatens the individual as much as collectivism ever did.

But that one impossible downward journey, that completely unselfish life, can found community wherever it moves an individual towards unselfishness.

Surrounded as we are by self-absorption, and a political ethic which promotes it, we experience a strong mimetic desire to imitate it. But Jesus' impossible journey provides something else to imitate. Many lives have been changed by a small book of that title, *The Imitation of Christ*. The central idea is the losing of the self in the mystery of Jesus' downward journey. So community can be based simply upon a shared wonder at the mystery of the cross.

There are two parables in the gospel that express God's inalienable love of the individual — the lost sheep and the prodigal son.

For us humans, sheep are a metaphor for community because of their instinctive tendency to stick together. Yet the search for food will often lead one sheep away from the herd. This is even more true of humans—concern for the self, one's own individual destiny, leads one away from community. This was never more true than today, when the slogan 'no free lunch' summarises the essential values of the market economy, and when successful education is the essential basis for material independence. The modern reliance upon the individual's economic independence is the most powerful spur to the individual's upward journey. Self-esteem comes to be associated with this independence, so that those who don't or can't find it are often treated with contempt, and feel contempt for themselves. This creates a profound problem for community, for such people naturally find an outlet for their alienation in anti-social activities such as crime or addiction.

The gospel identifies the Christian God as one who goes in search of such people. Yet who is to do the searching? Who is to heal the divisions in society caused by the exclusively upward journey of people in general, by communicating the truth that the individual is of infinite value, irrespective of his inability or unwillingness to climb the pyramid? The history of Christianity indicates the effectiveness of the crucifixion in unlocking the spirit of self-sacrifice in the individual, so that God again becomes incarnate and goes looking for the lost sheep. True conversion becomes self-sacrificial, healing the wounds of community.

This parable is a metaphor also for the individual's search for personal truth in a world that tells him, as Pilate did Christ, that truth is impossible to find. The truth lived by Jesus, to the last drop of blood, was the concern of the author of all creation for the individual human being. When we are deeply touched by that truth we are not merely ourselves reconciled, we become a means of reconciling others.

The parable of the prodigal son has a similar meaning. The father allows the younger son his freedom as he heads off into the world to seek his destiny. The son discovers the harshness of the world: good company can be bought as long as the money lasts, but the selfishness of men will guarantee a day of reckoning—the famine of the parable. The son has no alternative but abject return, hoping only for employment.

But the father sees him a long way off, which suggests he has never stopped scanning the horizon. Then he does not wait for the son to take those last steps of submission, but runs to him, and gathers him in an embrace that ignores his filthy condition. The older son of the parable, who is angry at the father's reception of the prodigal, is brother also to those who complain about equal pay to the latecomers in the vineyard; he has never left home, and so has never suffered—and so has not experienced the full depth of the Father's love. He is also therefore the successful individual who resents any show of concern for the lost individual—the personification of the man who has 'made it' and who cannot find compassion for those who have not.

In the younger son also we can find the passionate liberal who resents authority and emphasises the need for personal freedom. The father does not stand in his way, thus accepting the son's freedom. When the resources funding this freedom have been exhausted, the father is still there, waiting. The son has realised that freedom cannot be an end in itself.

And isn't this the essential truth of individual experience in our own time? When everyone insists upon his rights without considering his responsibilities, who is to secure those rights? A low-tax regime is desirable for those on the upward journey, but can it be reconciled with the low-crime society they also tend to demand? Here again the individual can be his own worst enemy. Those who take more than they give will destroy the world unless they are at least balanced by those who give more than they take. It is the latter life that Jesus honours, by living it to the last extremity.

So this gospel will never cease to be relevant to the problems of us humans. For all time it will address any society based upon the notion that people are unequal in dignity. It speaks to the individual heart, promoting self-sacrifice as well as reconciliation. It is therefore a living basis of local and global community, insisting upon the reality that we are all equal, and can never lose that equality in the sight of God. It says to us 'Your freedom is sacred, but can you use it in imitation of the one who gives it to you, to secure the freedom of others?' This question goes to the heart of our present predicament.

In the impossible journey of Christ we encounter a God passionately committed to the dignity of the individual. We also encounter an attempt to break the individual's heart, challenging the selfishness that springs from individual self-absorption.

Community begins where one person's compassion meets another's need. True freedom is the freedom to love and to serve. When it is exercised in this way—in the way of the Father—the world can be changed. This is the mustard seed planted everywhere by the foot of the cross.

CHAPTER X

Bridging the Chasm within the Church

The shortest-lived pope of the twentieth century, John Paul I, found time to say the following:

> A little more than a hundred years have passed since the decline of the temporal power of the popes; otherwise I too would now be a pope-king, with an army of soldiers and perhaps a police force to protect the goods, the lands and the palaces of the popes. How beautiful it would have been if the pope had himself voluntarily renounced all temporal power! He should have done it first. Let us give thanks to the Lord who has willed it and has done it.[23]

This statement has importance for a number of reasons.

First, it is an acknowledgement of the historical significance of the present era for the church, one in which it has finally lost most of the worldly power which it acquired in the fourth century, and which the world again gradually took from it in the modern era. It is a fundamental repudiation of the Augustinian option in favour of temporal power as a means of building the kingdom of God. Second, it is a joyful acceptance of that disempowerment. Thirdly, it allows us to identify the nature of our own era—one in which the Christian, as Christian, is almost as powerless as he was prior to the Constantinian conversion.

Worldly power allows us to command others in the knowledge that we will be obeyed. Powerless, we cannot do so. We are obliged to act in fellowship with one another. It is clear from the gospels that Jesus did not sort the apostles into a hierarchy of importance and esteem, and that this caused them problems: hierarchy of esteem was natural in the ancient world. His command was 'love one another as I have loved you'. His love was expressed above all in his invitation of his followers into the sonship and daughtership of the Father. That wondrous fellowship should be the chief characteristic of the church, not the pyramid of esteem and power it also became for so long.

Another implication of the pope's statement is that the church can no longer develop by wielding worldly power. The era when the conversion of rulers overawed by Christendom was followed automatically by conversion of those they ruled, is long gone. That era spoke also of the worldly power of the church, and it was to this power that many of its converts bowed, rather than to the wondrous fellowship of the church's founder.

We have arrived, in other words, at a point of supreme vulnerability, for we have lost control of the future. Or rather we have lost the illusion of control.

Augustine seized the moment of worldly empowerment of the church in the fourth century to envisage a global Christian empire. The church spent a millennium following that illusion, and then another half millennium defending it, never giving an inch, as John Paul I acknowledged. God clearly does not want the church to control the earth. God's programme is liberation, not control, so the conscious powerlessness of the Christian is an asset in communicating this truth.

It is an era of vulnerability, in which the Christian has no option other than to serve, in a world full of lost individuals who have tried and failed to climb the pyramid of esteem. It falls to the church, and to all men of good will who can understand the downward journey, to offer to these what Christ offered—an unearthly dignity in fellowship in which the pyramid of esteem has been banished.

The struggle for power

Jesus' downward journey took him to a position of extreme vulnerability, and it is still essentially this vulnerability that draws us to him. It is, therefore, inappropriate that there should ever be a struggle for power within the church. The power of the Christian is the power that Christ deliberately demonstrated at the last supper—the power to serve. We know from the gospel of St Luke that at that meal there was another of those paroxysms of jealousy among the apostles, another attempt to establish, while Jesus was still with them, a pyramid of esteem. So Jesus' washing of their feet is likely to have been a deliberate response. Even if not, the passage will have an eternal significance, for as long as we humans continue to build the pyramid.

Resolving the Problem of Clericalism

It is true that, in the Tridentine era, the Catholic clergy was given a virtual monopoly of leadership, liturgy and initiative in the church, and that most Catholics came to identify the church with this clergy. The role of the lay Catholic was generally passive and compliant, conditioned to thinking of the cleric as in all ways more competent in the articulation, celebration and application of the faith. It is also true that there are those in the church who wish to maintain this pyramid of esteem and competence, contrary to the spirit of Vatican II. However, the disempowerment of the clerical church nevertheless continues, compelling us to take thought of how a declericalised church can survive.

Careful study reveals that an omni-competent clergy, responsible for the maintenance and culture of the church, was unknown to the early Christians. Excluded from Temple and synagogue, their 'sacrifice', their 'altar', their 'temple', their 'priest' were Christ, and they shared in this priesthood through baptism and the sacrifice of their own lives. They used a non-priestly vocabulary to identify their leading ministers: episcopus, presbyter, deacon. Only in the course of time did the terms bishop and priest come to supplant the first two of these, and to define a clerical elite distinct from the laity.

Two things are clear from this: the need to enhance the spirit of fellowship between priest and people, and to remove the barriers to this that exist; and the need to spread the burden of conscious responsibility more widely, while maintaining continuity with the best aspects of the clerical system. The appointment of lay ministers of the Eucharist and lay readers is an important step in this direction, but there is still a heavy and dangerous reliance upon the theological, pastoral, administrative and liturgical expertise of the celibate priest—an endangered species nowadays. This is an important aspect of the crisis that faces the church.

However, in this crisis we are all free to serve in some ways, if not in all. The most important service we can all give, no matter what our rank and education, is to communicate the abiding love of the author of all life for all individuals, no matter what their worldly status, lay or clerical.

It is in the washing of the feet—that is, in service—that the power of God is exercised. We must all aspire to that service, not simply wait for a change of personnel and policy at the summit of the ecclesiastical pyramid. If the word 'ministry' means service, every Christian is a minister.

It follows from all of this that the lay Christian, male and female, living in the world, is at the leading edge of the church's development in the twenty-first century. Our lives are lived vulnerably in the world, giving us an understanding of its nature and of its general heartlessness. We live among the casualties of the upward journey, and can recognise them as equal children of the Father. These are the lost sheep of the new millennium. There will be many of them—the bitter, the cynical, the disillusioned, the addicted, the uneducated. The church was intended for all of these, and only the laity can effectively communicate this truth.

It is, above all, our privilege to welcome these casualties into a joyful fellowship marked by equal esteem, irrespective of the history of individuals. All of us must take most seriously the parable of the vineyard whose owner pays all of the workers the same at the end of the day. Those who are already joyfully in the kingdom should not mind in the least that their reward is the same as for those who have just entered. The owner is the Lord, whose company they will have known for a little longer; the work they do is the communication of this joy to those outside—and the reward for all at the end of the day is the company of the Lord forever.

CHAPTER XI

Futile Desire

In January 1999, the UK's *Sunday Times* revealed that there were two separate projects ongoing to build a supersonic executive jet, 'the ultimate in executive playthings'. Flying at twice the speed of sound and likely to cost $50 million per unit, this craft is designed to appeal to the fabulously wealthy—film stars, oil billionaires, computing entrepreneurs. A spokesman for one of the firms concerned was reported as saying 'The next holy grail of business travel is speed. You can always make improvements, but supersonic is the next big leap.'

The metaphor 'holy grail' reminds us of a time when our civilisation situated its understanding of heroism in a biblical context. King Arthur's knights supposedly went in search of the 'holy grail', the chalice that Jesus used at the last supper, offering it to his apostles with the words 'this is my blood'. No more. Now the summit of human achievement is the acquisition of vastly expensive products of technology. By 2006, we are assured, such planes will routinely fly across the great oceans of the world at speeds of up to 1500 miles per hour.

It is the exclusiveness of this experience which will make this plane the ultimate object of desire. Already there is a supersonic jet, Concorde, now thirty years old, but it is open to fare-paying passengers. And it does not have on board a sauna which, we are told, exists on the executive jet belonging to Tom Cruise and Nicole Kidman. The notion of exclusiveness is essential for ultimate objects of desire.

The reason for this is that once we humans satisfy our basic needs for food, shelter and security, our desires are heavily influenced by our need to possess at least those things that others possess; and particularly by our need to own what is possessed by those people we see as particularly successful or important. Possessions become symbols of status. The pyramid of esteem becomes a pyramid of ownership, with those at the summit owning objects which must be exclusive, because otherwise their status will be in doubt.

It follows that, since our economies are now based upon mass production, we become endlessly acquisitive. The shopping mall, the sales catalogue and the Internet offer us a multitude of desirable objects, and we succumb globally.

And so our homes become deposits of a myriad of possessions, and we should be happy — as happy as those who possess nothing suppose we must be. Not so. What we possess almost instantly becomes 'stuff', and we regard it with ennui. In the United States there are people who make a living as consultants on the problem of accumulating 'stuff'. They will visit your home and tell you how to organise it. If necessary they will advise on storage facilities outside the home — space you can rent to store the 'stuff' you can presently find no use for.

Why this ennui? Because the semi-magical aura of the desired object disappears as soon as it has been bought and admired. Our peers are acquiring the same objects, so our status in the pyramid has not changed. Why not give them away, then? Because their loss will diminish our status. Soon it will be time for another bout of acquisition, another 'fix'.

But endless desire is futile also, because the upward journeys of those climbing the pyramid of esteem are constantly ratcheting upwards the cost of what is most exclusive. If supersonic executive jets become anyway plentiful, something more exclusive will be developed. Soon enough, someone will propose the building of personal space shuttles which will ferry people to exclusive space hotels where one can enjoy the exclusive experience of intimate weightlessness. There will always be desires that most of us cannot fulfil, and this will intensify our desire, unless we can recognise and nullify it.

The Power of Mimetic Desire

The advertising industry well understands the power of mimetic desire—the need to have what prestigious people have. On the inside front cover of *Time* magazine there is typically an advertisement for watches that cost thousands of dollars. The sales pitch is that one of the world's top sports personalities already has one of these, and would never be without it because of its peerless reliability. Such ads are fixtures, testimony to the power of mimetic desire. They are expensive, and would not be bought if the watches were unsold, even though perfectly reliable watches can be bought for a small fraction of their price. Certain marques of cars too are sold for their associations with people of status—in terms of mechanical superiority their price is entirely unjustified.

The need to be aware of mimetic desire is obvious, for many reasons:

An inability to indulge it is often a pointless reason for self-dislike and self-destruction.

It offers only the illusion of fulfilment. Deep in the human heart there is a perception that mimetic desire is essentially stupid, a fundamental human flaw.

People are valuable to society in terms of their unselfishness, not their ability to indulge their desires.

It is the root of envy, and is therefore destructive of human relationships.

It can be a serious cause of conflict. The Falklands war, like many others in history, was fought essentially due to mimetic desire for territory of extremely questionable importance. Political nationalism is essentially mimetic desire for exclusive possession of real estate.

It prevents the transfer of sufficient human resources to peoples dying of want.

It cannot be environmentally sustained. To fulfil the mimetic desires of the world's present population, in particular the desires of the developing world for the lifestyle of the developed world, the resources of several other planets of the same size would be required, and even then all must become landfill sites in time.

The argument for endless desire

Those for whom the market is sovereign will argue that it is human acquisitiveness that supports the standard of living of the west. Yet the growing 'voluntary simplicity' movement argues far more persuasively that the equation of wealth with possessions is the fundamental source of the deterioration of vital relationships, particularly those within the family. More and more people are choosing to earn less, consume less, and spend more time together. Uncontrolled mimetic desire, it seems clear, robs people of their most valuable possession—time—and the wave of the future will be to reclaim it. It used to be argued that mass production would lead to lives of leisure. It was the market, constantly stimulating the appetite for possessions, that nullified this dream. It is time to revive it, but no such attempt will be successful until we can perceive that the desires by which we are manipulated are linked spiritually with the upward journey.

Mimetic Desire and the Downward Journey

In the bible, mimetic desire is called covetousness, and two of the ten commandments are devoted to it: we must covet neither our neighbour's goods nor his wife. Probably the term fell into disuse because we have become almost blind to its power over us. Mass production is one reason for this—our economies clone many objects of desire in vast quantities, holding out the prospect of desire without conflict. Yet our rediscovery of the concept is crucial to the future of humanity.

It is only in the downward journey that we can identify mimetic desire in our own perceived needs, monitor its power over us, and resist its most destructive effects. This too is a spiritual gift that the Judaeo-Christian tradition can recover for us, if we simply obey the first commandment, which is the love of God above all else. Jesus fought and conquered mimetic desire, and it is in the imitation of Christ that we too will find deliverance from it. This is why the giving away of surplus wealth carries with it more spiritual benefit than the acquisition of it. The life that was simply given away, celebrated every Sunday, should be, for Christians in the developed world, the spur to a fundamental, world-changing generosity.

CHAPTER XII

Coming to the Father

Genesis is unerring in describing the primary and original sin: Satan tempted us with the promise: 'You will be as Gods.'

For all men in all cultures, Gods are at the summit of the pyramid of power and esteem. They are immortal and above all want and pain. They are also worshipped, which is what we think we want for ourselves. And so we set out upon the upward journey, using whatever gifts we may have.

This is 'the world', in which all seek glory from one another.

But glory is the gift of the many to the very few, so few can receive it. So the upward journey is futile for most of us. We can be no more than extras in the epic film, spectators and worshippers of the few. Our lives are lived in envy of theirs, watching TV or scanning the magazine racks.

And for those few the upward journey is usually worse than futile. They are trapped in the role or image that has won them glory, and live in a glass bowl of media fascination. Well aware of their own weaknesses, they live in fear of exposure, of becoming yesterday's idols. Their success cannot buy what they soon come to value most, their own seclusion and privacy.

Yet the rest of us have all the privacy we want, and see it as evidence of relative failure. What can be the purpose of this brief life if not to be as Gods—if only for a day?

And so we climb from one day to the next, and so the world is a wilderness of upward journeys in which dissatisfaction and selfishness rule most lives. In looking up we have no time for the less fortunate. Consequently many, many lives are lived in the sadness of self-dislike. If the world cannot recognise us, must not we be 'losers', people who have failed?

Not so. The purpose of this life is to help people come back to the Father, with whom we once walked and talked as children in Eden, and by whom each of us is still infinitely and equally loved. And Jesus will take us to him.

Am I really serious? Do I really believe in a personal God, a being separate and independent of our own thoughts, who is interested in us as individuals, and with whom we can communicate?

And I answer: Yes, Yes, Yes! This is the good news! There is a marvellous truth in Christianity greater than any that science fiction has yet dreamed of. There is such a being who loves each of us equally and infinitely, with whom we can commune. Those who are still happy on the upward journey have no need of him, do not experience him, and can safely discount his existence.

Yet those who are in pain or desolation and cry out to him will not be left unanswered, if they meditate upon the Son, and upon his extraordinary downward journey to reach them.

I have called this journey extraordinary because in worldly terms it makes no sense. We know the names of very few of all whom our world has crucified. Crassus did indeed buy immortality by hanging the 6,000, and their names have been forgotten forever by the world. So we should know nothing of Jesus either. His downward journey should have meant his extinction. Who, in his right mind, would undertake such a journey?

There is no doubt that he was in his right mind. From the start he was beset by men who set out to trap him, and answered with a peerless self-possession and intelligence. There is not a hint of fanaticism or mental imbalance.

There is also his disregard for the Temple system, which had created a spiritual pyramid of esteem that condemned the poor to a sense of hopelessness because they could not afford the means of winning forgiveness. This was bound to antagonise powerful people. Why do so? Why spend time and fellowship with the condemned and excluded? What good was their company when they were shunned by the virtuous? Why seek out Zacchaeus and Bartimaeus, the tax shark and the blind man? Why this elevation of unworthy individuals to his company when this would alienate many of the good people who could have praised him otherwise?

Because the purpose of the downward journey is to recognise all individuals without exception, to raise them into the company of by far the greatest man who ever lived. And to convince them of the Father's love.

If we doubt the existence of the Father, then this journey to Calvary becomes entirely inexplicable. If we accept that for Jesus the Father was an ever-present reality, we can see this journey as the Father's revelation of himself. Either way, we are presented with a mystery, but belief in the unity of Father and Son changes people profoundly.

Always, down through time, Jesus has drawn to himself people who have a rare gift. Throughout those many centuries when the church leadership often abused its power, there have been people who balanced that fault with lives of self-diminishment and service: St Antony, who went back to the desert to find the Father whom Jesus loved, founding the hermitical tradition; St Benedict, who created a rule of life for monks living in community, sowing the seed of monasticism which kept alive the tradition of unselfishness and scholarship throughout the Middle Ages, as well as establishing the first hospitals; St Francis, whose followers took up the challenge of poverty, helping to prove the love of God for the poorest during the darkest times; St Ignatius Loyola, whose conversion in the course of recovery from a war wound led to the foundation of the Jesuits, still today affirming the dignity of the poorest in the barrios of Latin America; St Teresa of Avila, whose passion for God still draws people to the mystical life; St Therese of Lisieux whose search for a 'little way' to

God, while dying of tuberculosis, led her also to the downward journey, influencing many in this twentieth century to do the same.

In our own time, Jean Vanier, founder of the *L'Arche* communities in which the mentally disabled are tended by able people on the spiritual journey, identifies exactly the same truth:

> The poor and the weak have revealed to me the great secret of Jesus. If you wish to follow him you must not try to climb the ladder of success and power, becoming more and more important. Instead, you must walk down the ladder, to meet and walk with people who are broken and in pain. The light is there, shining in the darkness, in the darkness of their poverty. The poor with whom you are called to share your life are perhaps the sick and the old; people out of work, young people caught up in the world of drugs, people angry because they were terribly hurt when they were young, people with disabilities or sick with Aids, or just out of prison; people in slums or ghettos, people in far-off lands where there is much hunger and suffering, people who are oppressed because of the colour of their skin, people who are lonely in overcrowded cities, people in pain.[24]

Christ is the way to the Father for he obeyed him completely, and gifted to all of us sisterhood and brotherhood in the Father's love. In the downward journey he draws to himself all who are abused by the world, all who are ignored, all who see themselves as failures, all who are in the grip of an addiction. In our baptism we are recognised as sons and daughters of the Father, and can never lose this status.

How do we experience the Father's love? First, travel with Jesus on his journey, seeing it as a journey in search of yourself. In your own pain, see the pain of the Son. See also that although this world sets out to enslave you in self-dislike, Jesus sets out to draw you to him by disempowering himself. He knows that you can come freely to him only in love, and so dies without empowering himself to demand that love. He has been ill-served by those who would compel—they simply do not understand the downward journey.

This truth you may come across in unexpected places. Here, Huckleberry Finn, rafting down the Mississippi with the runaway black slave Jim, has a sudden attack of white middle class morality which leads him to write a letter to Jim's 'owner':

> *Miss Watson, Your runaway nigger Jim is down here two mile below Pikesville, and Mr. Phelps has got him and he will give him up for the reward if you send.—Huck Finn*
>
> I felt good and all washed clean of sin for the first time I had ever felt so in my life, and I knowed I could pray now. But I didn't do it straight off, but laid the paper down and set there thinking—thinking how good it was all this happened so, and how near I come to being lost and going to hell. And went on thinking. And got to thinking over our trip down the river; and I see Jim before me all the time: in the day and in the night-time, sometimes moonlight, sometimes storms, and we a-floating along, talking and singing and laughing. But somehow I couldn't seem to strike no places to harden me against him, but only the other kind. I'd see him standing my watch on top of his'n, 'stead of calling me, so I could go on sleeping; and see him how glad he was when I come back out of the fog; and when I come to him again in the swamp, up there where the feud was; and suchlike times; and would always call me honey, and pet me and do everything he could think of for me, and how good he always was; and at last I struck the time I saved him by telling the men we had smallpox aboard, and he was so grateful, and said I was the best friend old Jim ever had in the world, and

the ONLY one he's got now; and then I happened to look around and see that paper.

It was a close place. I took it up, and held it in my hand. I was a-trembling, because I'd got to decide, forever, betwixt two things, and I knowed it. I studied a minute, sort of holding my breath, and then says to myself:

'All right, then, I'll GO to hell'—and tore it up.
It was awful thoughts and awful words, but they was said. And I let them stay said; and never thought no more about reforming. I shoved the whole thing out of my head, and said I would take up wickedness again, which was in my line, being brung up to it, the other warn't. And for a starter I would go to work and steal Jim out of slavery again; and if I could think up anything worse, I would do that, too; because as long as I was in, and in for good, I might as well go the whole hog.[25]

Going to hell for someone is the essence of the gospel story, and an eternally subversive choice. Mark Twain declared that anyone foolish enough to find a moral in his novel would be banished, but here we find unmistakable signs of the impact of the Gospel, intuitively, upon the understanding of freedom in western consciousness. The Father who planted this notion is not the authoritarian parent for whom order is preferred to liberty.

Notice here that this moment is one of self-discovery for Huck—he's not one of the good folks who can think of a black man as someone's rightful property. He has to make a choice between respectability—what his social superiors will think of him—and what Jim will think of him. He has to choose between the upward and the downward journey. In choosing the latter he thinks he is alienating God, but is in fact finding him—and finding himself at the same time.

My own experience, and that of many people I know, is that the experience of the Father—that sense of his presence and his love—begins often in a time of great pain when we are forced to evaluate our lives, then turn prayerfully to the Son in his pain, and then remember it is always the Father who sends us the Son. And when we understand the unity of the Father and the Son, which is also the solidarity of the Creator with all of his creation, we will receive the Spirit. It is then we receive a life in union with the Trinity that is beyond all power of mine to describe.

Salvation—related to salutary (conducive to health)—is a word for it: a sense of completion and fulfilment and mental health that sees through all death to the eternal. I have no doubt that, in the downward journey of Jesus Christ, each of us can find our own salvation. Yet we will lose it if we keep it to ourselves. History shows conclusively that Christians cannot be mass produced. It is in the free choice of the downward journey—the recognition and prioritisation of the pain of others—that Jesus' journey goes on and on, and it is to this journey that each of us is called.

NOTES

1 René Girard, *Things Hidden Since the Foundation of the World*, Athlone Press, 1987

2 *Epistle of Mathetes to Diognetus*, Ante-Nicene Fathers

3 Paul Johnson, *A History of Christianity*, Penguin Books,1976, p.76

4 Ibid., p. 77

5 St Ambrose, *Epistle XVIII*, Nicene and Post-Nicene Fathers

6 St Augustine of Hippo, *Epistle XXIII*, P.L., XXXIII, 98

7 St Augustine of Hippo, P.L., XXXII, 632

8 St Augustine of Hippo, on Psalm XCVI, Nicene and Post-Nicene Fathers, Vol. 8

9 St Augustine of Hippo, Letter CLXXIII, Nicene and Post-Nicene Fathers, Vol. 1

10 Ibid.

11 Ibid.

12 Quoted in Paul Johnson, op. cit., p. 244

13 Quoted in T. Jones & A. Areira, Crusades, p. 52

14 Ibid., p. 52

15 Ibid., p. 53

16 *Polycraticus*, 1. IV, P.L., 119, 516

17 Quoted in Paul Johnson, op. cit., p. 252

18 W.B. Yeats, 'The Second Coming', *Collected Poems*

19 Pope Pius IX, *Syllabus of Errors*, 1864

20 The Documents of Vatican II, *Declaration on Religious Freedom*, Introduction

21 J. Courtney Murray, *We Hold These Truths: Catholic Reflections on the American Proposition*, 1964

22 Joseph Cardinal Ratzinger, *Salt of the Earth: Christianity and the Catholic Church at the End of the Millennium, An Interview with Peter Seewald*, Ignatius press, 1997

23 Quoted in Luigi Accattoli, *When a Pope asks Forgiveness: The Mea Culpas of John Paul II*, Alba House, 1998, p. 44

24 Jean Vanier, *The Broken Body*, Darton, Longman and Todd, 1988, p. 72

25 Mark Twain, *Huckleberry Finn*, Chapter XXXI

GLOSSARY

ambivalence

A tendency to think about the same thing in contradictory ways.

agnosticism

The belief that the existence of God can be neither proven nor disproven, and that life must therefore be lived without commitment to either position.

anticlericalism

Antagonism towards, and opposition to the influence of, clerics, particularly in the intellectual and political spheres.

apotheosis

Becoming a God — the climax of the human upward journey in the ancient world.

chasm

A chasm is a deep opening in the earth. Here the word is used to describe a lack of follow-through in human intentions and aspirations, so that human undertakings remain unfulfilled. It has both a social and an individual dimension.

Christendom

The union of church and state that followed the conversion of the Roman Emperor Constantine to Christianity in 313 AD. By the end of the fourth century Christianity was the state religion, and by the eleventh century the church dominated the most powerful Christian rulers of Europe.

Crusades

Christian expeditions from western Europe to the near east to recapture 'the holy lands' (Palestine) from Islamic rule. The five most important crusades fell between 1095 and 1221 AD.

clericalism

A belief in the social and / or intellectual and / or moral superiority of clerics—those with a specifically religious and theological role and professional expertise.

consumerism

The promotion of a consumer society in which people are valued for their spending power.

corruption

In political life this involves accepting bribes to use influence to benefit the giver.

dogma

A belief or beliefs held to be essential and binding.

downward journey

A life centred upon the need to recognise, help, and value others, particularly the less fortunate. It involves the rejection of an 'upward journey' focused upon the self.

egalitarianism

The belief that all humans are equal in dignity.

'The Enlightenment'

A movement of ideas originating in the excitement over Newton's discovery of the universal natural laws of gravitation and motion, published in the 1680s. Voltaire, and other eighteenth century writers who popularised Newton's ideas, believed that the methods of science would eventually explain everything by discovering the 'natural laws' which governed all phenomena, and then apply these laws to improve society, rendering the churches obsolete and irrelevant. The 'Enlightenment' rejected the idea of original sin, holding that proper understanding and education would enable people to act wisely. It secularised thought and society in Catholic Europe, wresting control of these from clerics, who tended to condemn it. The 'Enlightenment' was thus the main source of modern secularism, and of modernism.

entrepreneur

One who is gifted in making money by spotting opportunities and then exploiting them.

fundamentalism

A tendency to reduce religious truth to principles said to be basic or fundamental. In Christianity it also involves a protective attitude to the bible, read literally. For example, a biblical fundamentalist might insist that the creation of the world did indeed take place in the six days specified in Genesis. This implies a belief that the bible was written by God, dictating every word to human scribes, and that God too is a literalist. As Jesus is quoted as saying 'I am the vine and you are the branches', it seems that God is more intelligent than this.

genocide

> The attempt to murder a racial or ethnic group.

hierarchy

> Here, the pyramid of esteem, the ranking of humans into a pyramid in which those few at the summit are deemed more important than the majority who make up the base.

ideology

> A body of ideas that supposedly justifies and explains a policy or attitude. Here the term is used specifically to denote grandiose political theories such as communism, nationalism, etc.

inclusiveness

> A policy of leaving no-one out—here particularly outside the love and recognition of God.

individualism

> An attitude dominated by self-interest, in which community values are disregarded

Inquisition

> General name for a system of courts set up by the Catholic Church to investigate and punish what were believed to be false ideas (or heresy) dangerous to true faith. They functioned from the thirteenth to the nineteenth centuries AD.

Internet

> The system of telephone, satellite and cable communication that allows the world's computers to interact with one another, using other computers dedicated to this purpose.

liberal agenda

> The policies associated with liberalism. Opponents of liberalism use this as a derogatory term for a residual agenda consisting of sexual freedoms not yet achieved in some societies—a free choice on abortion, legal recognition of homosexual relationships, etc. The full liberal agenda in western society consists also of basic political and intellectual freedoms, which conservative Catholics now accept and make use of, although our church opposed them when first promoted.

liberalism

> The belief that the freedom of the individual to determine his own beliefs and express them publicly is of the utmost importance. Liberals believe also that people should be free to organise themselves politically, in a democratic political system.

Marxism-Leninism

> The ideology of the communist party in the Soviet Union from 1917-1989, based supposedly upon the idea of state ownership of all wealth for the good of all. Essentially it simply justified the total power of the Communist party.

meritocracy

> A community in which people are valued and promoted on supposed merit, rather than on, say, family connections.

mimesis

> The human gift (and scourge) of unconscious imitation. It is exploited by advertisers when they associate their product (e.g. the Rolex watch) with famous people. This is designed to arouse mimetic desire—a subconscious belief that 'I need' a Rolex watch.

mimetic desire

> The subconsciously acquired desire to possess something someone else possesses. In the bible it is called 'covetousness'. See also mimesis.

modernism

> An attitude originating with the eighteenth-century 'Enlightenment' which generally regarded religion as a source of intolerance and violence, and proposed to build a new rational world on the findings and applications of science and technology. The term is also used to describe a theological movement to adapt Christianity to modern values such as democracy and equality. The idea of progress is embedded in both understandings of modernism. See also post-modernism.

narcissism

> Narcissus was a character in Greek mythology who fell in love with his own reflection.

nationalism

> The belief that nations should be free and self-governing within a designated national territory. Thus an Irish nationalist wants to belong to an independent Irish state, outside the control of the United Kingdom. Nationalism typically confronts the problem of minorities who do not identify with the majority in a given territory, provoking violence and/or displacement.

natural law

> This term has two quite different meanings here. The first relates to the scientific laws which govern natural phenomena. For example: 'to every action there is an equal and opposite reaction'. For Newton and the Enlightenment this was a law of nature,

applying everywhere in the universe. It was the business of science to discover such laws.

The second meaning of 'natural law' relates to moral laws which can arguably be discerned by the use of reason, for example, the wrongness of murder. This is the sense in which the church normally uses the term, to justify a particular moral stance. Some authorities derive the principle of religious freedom from this understanding of 'natural law'.

orthodoxy

Catholic teaching as expounded by, e.g. the *Catechism of the Catholic Church*.

philosophes

The leaders of the eighteenth century 'Enlightenment', e.g. Voltaire.

pyramid of esteem

The conception of a given society or organisation as having 'important' people at the top and 'unimportant' people—the majority—at the base. The upward journey is the attempt to climb the pyramid of esteem one holds in one's own head. Here it is argued that such pyramids are human misconceptions, challenged by the life and death of Jesus Christ whose purpose it was to convince us that we are all equally esteemed by the Creator of all life.

post-modernism

A questioning of the optimism of modernism. It is pessimistic about the possibility of moral and social progress, and about the human intellectual capacity to be certain of anything. It is therefore a reaction against the Enlightenment, but without necessarily reverting to a religious view of life. The term is unsatisfactory, both because of its largely negative implications and because it creates a problem of naming whatever will succeed it. See also 'modernism'.

reason

Here the use of observation, experiment, maths or logic to provide a foundation for belief, rejecting faith—a reliance on an unverifiable divine revelation. The 'Enlightenment' believed that reason would reveal all truth and create a perfect world, and that faith based upon divine revelation or the authority of the church was irrational. However, the continual use of reason to demolish the foundations of all systems of belief has reached its natural terminus in the argument that truth is unattainable even by reason.

scapegoating violence

The human tendency to pick a weak target for chaotic aggression that might otherwise destroy an entire community. It focuses all aggression upon a victim or victims, reuniting the community in that aggressive cause. Some anthropologists theorise that this is the way in which culture and religion become established.

secularisation

The process whereby knowledge and social control were de-clericalised following the Enlightenment—that is, removed from clerical control and placed in the hands of non-clerics. Secularisation also tends to exclude religious ideas and language, on the presumption that they are irrelevant to a discourse based exclusively on reason. Thus, the secularisation of education implies the removal of religious ideas, language and symbols.

secularism

> An attitude and ideology that argues against any reference to religious or spiritual values or concepts in the formulation of public policy or in the educational system. A thoroughgoing secularism argues against the teaching of religion in schools, for example, arguing that public education must be exclusively practical and utilitarian. Secularism is also usually antagonistic to the influence of clerics, and so is anticlerical. Notice that secularism, an attitude or movement, is not quite the same thing as secularisation, a process.

spin doctor

> In politics someone who is knowledgeable about what a majority like to hear from their politicians, and who tailors the speeches of politicians accordingly. In so doing, he or she is putting a particular 'spin' upon a policy to make it palatable.

upward journey

> The individual's search for fulfilment in the approval or adulation of other humans, in the belief that their valuation is all-important. See also pyramid of esteem.

Utopia

> St Thomas More's name for a fictional island, the home of his ideal society, described in a book of the same title (1516 CE). Meaning literally 'Nowhere' in Greek, it is used generally to denote a perfect society which we can seek or describe but never realise.

West

> Shorthand for the cultures rimming the north Atlantic, principally western Europe and North America. They share a common cultural heritage, once based upon Christianity but now seriously confused.